The Restoration of
Leominster Priory Church

Sir George Gilbert Scott

Rev. Augustin Gaspard Edouart

and the

Restoration of
Leominster Priory Church

by
Eric Turton

The Friends of Leominster Priory
in association with
Logaston Press

LOGASTON PRESS
Little Logaston Woonton Almeley
Herefordshire HR3 6QH
logastonpress.co.uk

First published in 2006

ISBN 1 904396 60 7
(978 1 904396 60 4)

Set in Baskerville and Times by Logaston Press
and printed in Great Britain by
The Cromwell Press, Trowbridge

*This book is dedicated
to my long-suffering Wife,
Family and Friends*

Contents

Acknowledgements

This account owes its existence to a course I studied in 1998. The course was one organised by The University of Birmingham School of Continuing Studies and was entitled *Picturesque to Arts & Crafts: Landscape and Architecture*. The tutor was David Whitehead, a lecturer I had known for some years and whose previous courses I had attended. As we had been studying Sir G.G. Scott in connection with his restoration of Hereford cathedral, and knowing a little about his connection with Leominster priory church, I decided to make his restoration of that church the subject for my second assignment. He gave me an 'A' grade and commented 'You have produced something original – another Leominster History Society pamphlet or possibly Woolhope Transactions?' My connection with Leominster Folk Museum, where I had been curator for some years, had given me access to numerous photographs, a few documents, and the collected copies of the *Leominster News* (now fortunately available on microfilm in Leominster Library). My brother, W. Denis Turton, was not only a local solicitor and Superintendent Registrar, but was the direct successor to Edwin Lloyd, who plays an important part in this story. He was the founder chairman of both the Museum and the Leominster History Society, the latter post I had the honour to hold twenty-five years after its foundation. He provided me with access to significant documents such as the faculty for the erection of the gallery built in the church in 1756.

Thanks to my association with both the museum and the history society I made the acquaintance of the then Leominster Librarian, Peter Holliday, who not only provided considerable encouragement and friendship over the years, but also copies of the two photographs of the gutted church and of the sketches by W.H. Freeman (whom I originally confused with Edward Freeman).

I owe a special thanks to the late Ian Stair for his imaginative reconstruction of the Norman monastic church although, on the advice of Joe Hillaby, the historian, and with the permission of Ian, I have removed the anachronistic porch.

I also owe special thanks to Joe Hillaby both for general encouragement and for his work on the early history of the ecclesiastical establishment in Leominster. I am very grateful for his correcting some of my more glaring errors in Chapter 1.

A lot of my early research was carried out in the Hereford Record Office and I owe a lot to the help of Sue Hubbard and all the staff who work in that friendly institution. Most of the Leominster parish records, from which a large amount of my information has been culled, are held there, as are the Hereford Diocesan records concerning the Leominster Church.

The staff at both Leominster and Hereford libraries have always been an enormous help. I have already mentioned Peter Holliday and I must give special thanks to Robin Hill of Hereford library who, among many other things, provided all the information I needed about Rev. A.G. Edouart's father, rather like producing a rabbit out of a hat. Both libraries have been to endless trouble providing me with access to the three main newspapers from whose overlapping accounts I have been able to piece together a large part of the story together with access to early editions of Crockfords.

I must give very specific thanks to a number of institutions and individuals for permission to use material in their possession. The Royal Institute of British Architects gave me permission to use copies of Scott's original plans as well as the pages from his sketch-book dedicated to the Leominster Wheel of Life. I must also thank the Diocesan Registrar for obtaining the permission of the Bishop of Hereford to quote the documents relating to Rev. Hugh Reed, contained in boxes HD 10/20 and HD 10/22 in Hereford Record Office. I must also give thanks to Mr. A.C. James for giving permission to quote the Arkwright/Edouart correspondence ref. AS63/IV/9/26 in Hereford Record Office, and to Hereford Cathedral Library for providing the photograph of Rev. Edouart, ref. B – 6 – 15. The 1859 pencil sketch of Sir George Gilbert Scott (NPG2475) was provided by the National Portrait Gallery from their collection.

The remainder of the drawings and photographs are from the Leominster Folk Museum collection or are in my own possession as are some of the documents quoted.

Last, but very far from least, I must thank John Campbell who convinced me that I should turn my researches into a book that could be published in aid of the funds of the Friends of Leominster Priory.

Introduction

Leominster is a small market town in the centre of North Herefordshire. Although there is some archaeological evidence for Roman occupation it was really founded in about the year 660 as a religious settlement. The original settlement was on top of a rise in a bend in the River Lugg where its flow changes from east to south. A short distance downstream it is joined by a major tributary, the River Arrow, so the settlement was effectively bounded by water on three sides. With the exception of a northern suburb, the town has not spread beyond these fluvial limits.

North Herefordshire was known for religious non-conformity from the days of the Lollards in the early fifteenth century, for Sir John Oldcastle, one of their leaders and thought to be the model for Shakespeare's Sir John Falstaff, lived not far from Leominster.

By the late seventeenth century, even before the Act of Toleration of 1689, there were at least three dissenting bodies in Leominster including the Baptists and the Quakers. For this reason Lord Coningsby gave the town the nickname, *Little Amsterdam*. These were joined by the Presbyterians, the Congregationalists, Wesleyan Methodists, Primitive Methodists, Moravians and several smaller sects including the Llewelynites, an offshoot of the Presbyterian Church, led by the Rev. William Lewelyn. He was a friend of the Duke of Norfolk who had a house in the town. Rev. Lewelyn died in his pulpit in mid-sermon on Sunday, January 30th, 1803. Catholicism never died out in the area. Father Cadwallader was hung, drawn, and quartered in a rather amateurish fashion in Leominster in 1610, but being a Roman Catholic and a recusant did not stop John Able from receiving building contracts from both the state and the church, for he built Leominster's old Town-Hall and restored Dore Abbey. The Roman Catholic church was firmly re-established in Leominster in 1868 when the local Catholics bought the former Wesleyan Chapel in Burgess Street. The present church, designed by Peter Paul Pugin, was opened in 1888.

The Plymouth Brethren were well established in Leominster by the middle of the nineteenth century, and a number of small sects, such as Sydney Black's mission which he called the *Church of Christ* which occupied the old Wesleyan Chapel after the Roman Catholics had moved into their new church.

This broad and well-established non-conformist tradition had never been stronger in Leominster than during the second half of the nineteenth century. Several of the leading men in the town, such as the Southall and Newman families who were mainly responsible for a new water-supply and sanitation, the British School, and the Orphanage, were Quakers.

Religion and politics were closely linked, the non-conformists tending to support the Liberals, while the Conservatives were closely associated with the Anglican Church. Unfortunately violence occasionally entered into the picture, especially during the tenure of Rev. George Albert Rogers, who was Vicar of Leominster from 1847 until 1851. One of the people involved in the violence was Thomas Smith. He was landlord of the *Bunch of Grapes* and a drunkard, but later reformed and eventually became Canon of Bathurst Cathedral in Australia. He published his autobiography in 1856 where he describes several occurrences in which he was involved. These included the use of a hired mob to start a brawl at the opening of the infant-school and the statement 'Base attempts were constantly made against the vicar's life.' While some allowance must be made for the author's exaggerations, there is no doubt that Rev. Rogers was subject to several forms of persecution and these were referred to in one of the pamphlets published in 1864 written by Rev. A.G. Edouart.

During the period when the restoration of Leominster Priory Church was carried out, there was considerable opposition to the supremacy of the established Church. Fortunately there were some ecumenically minded people, such as the solicitor Edwin Lloyd, who were able partly to bridge the gap between the opposing sides. Unfortunately the landed gentry were entering a period of diminishing agricultural prices and reduced rental incomes and this applied to the leading landowners in the Leominster area, namely the Arkwrights of Hampton Court, the Batemans of Shobdon Court, and the Rodneys of Berrington Court. Of these only the Arkwrights seem to have provided much financial support to Leominster Priory Church.

So the story of the restoration of the ancient building is as much one of personalities as it is of actual repairs, for the whole exercise depended as much on the Vicar and the Johnny Arkwright, as it did on Sir George Gilbert Scott. Most of all it depended on the inhabitants of Leominster and friends of the ancient borough who contributed the funds that were eventually spent.

CHAPTER 1
RESTORATION – WHY WAS IT NECESSARY?

Visitors to Leominster Priory Church of St. Peter and St. Paul find a fascinating, but rather odd church. It seems to have three naves of roughly the same size, one rather detached from the others, and a north aisle. There is no real choir or chancel and the northern nave in particular has a rather truncated look. This nave is unmistakably Norman. It has a magnificent west door with carved capitals, but the measured march of the arches on either side is interrupted by strange blocks of masonry pierced by narrow arches. This nave with its northern aisle has a floor several feet lower than that of the rest of the church. The central nave is less easy to date, but its west window was inserted in about 1500. The southernmost nave seems to be about a century earlier with a series of ball-flower windows in the Decorated style. To make it more confusing the screen between the central and southern nave is 19th century in date, and the east windows of all three date from the 20th century, although the one at the east end of the Norman nave is a copy of the Norman window over the west door.

As with most buildings of this age and importance it has had a very varied history which has affected its appearance and led on more than one occasion to its near destruction but this account is an attempt to trace the history of its restoration which was begun in 1862 and continued with many interruptions for more than fifty years.

The earliest part of the present building dates from 1123 when the monastery and all its considerable lands were made a cell of Reading Abbey and a new church was built. This was consecrated in 1130 and was dedicated to St. Peter. It probably looked something like the reconstruction on the next page. At first glance it is a simple, cruciform, church with a central tower and an apsidal east end with five chapels. However, a look at the interior of the nave reveals a curious series of semicircular Norman arches interrupted by solid blocks of masonry each pierced by a narrow round headed arch. There are two of these blocks on each side of the nave, but it seems certain that there were originally three. Whatever the original purpose of these it seems to have been abandoned and the triforium immediately above has a simple series of arches which bear no relationship to those beneath.

The western tower seems to have been added not long after the nave was completed. Only the lower stage is mid-to-late 12th century and it contains the magnificent west door with its intricately carved capitals and the window above whose capitals are similarly carved. The upper stages are later and there is no evidence that they replaced any earlier construction.

The possible appearance of Leominster Priory Church in the 12th century

Another curiosity is that the alignments of the eastern and western parts of the church were not identical.

The cloisters and monastic buildings, some parts of which survive, lay to the north of the church.

The nave was for public worship, but early in the 13th century a possible breakdown between the parish and monastic authorities led to the romanesque South Aisle being replaced by a nave for the exclusive use of the parish which I will refer to as the Parish Nave. This was the church of St. Paul and was consecrated in 1239.

A century later, the Parish Nave proving to be too small, a South Aisle, or South Nave as it was often called, was added. The south wall of this new, Decorated, addition was notable for its five windows with their ball-flower decoration.

At the end of the 14th, or perhaps in the early years of the 15th century, a new perpendicular window replaced the original west window in the Parish Nave, probably at the expense of Lady Matilda Mowbray. The two upper stories of the tower were added at about the same time. This latter construction was done in a rather strange way that will be described in connection with the restoration of the tower.

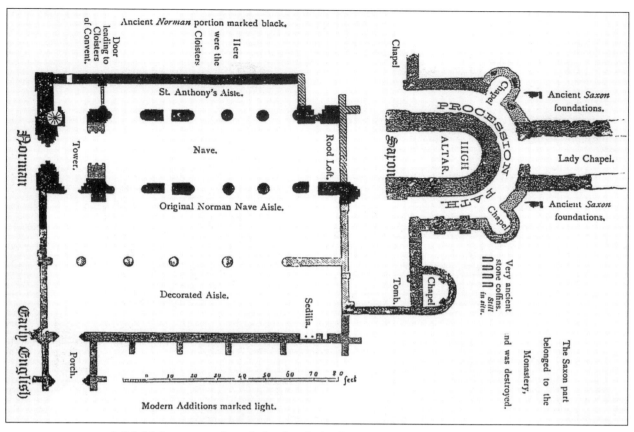

Ancient *Norman* portion marked black.

Door leading to Cloisters of Convent.

Here were the Cloisters

St. Anthony's Aisle.

Chapel

Ancient *Saxon* foundations.

PROCESSION PATH

SAXON

HIGH ALTAR.

Lady Chapel.

Ancient *Saxon* foundations.

Norman

Tower.

Nave.

Rood Loft.

Original Norman Nave Aisle.

Chapel

Very ancient stone coffins. *Still in situ.*

...nd was destroyed.

Tomb.

The Saxon part belonged to the Monastery,

Early English

Decorated Aisle.

Sedilia.

Porch.

0 10 20 30 40 50 60 70 8 0 feet

Modern Additions marked light.

Mid 19th-century plan of the church (copied from Rev. Edouart's History)

No major changes or additions seem to have been made to the existing part of the church before the monastery was suppressed in 1539.

The fact that the Priory Church and the Parish Church were parts of the same building meant that part of the former survived. It did not, however, save the eastern (monastic) end of the Priory Church as far west as the crossing which, like most of the Priory buildings, were used as a source of building stone. This was still the case nearly a hundred years later for there is an entry in the Chamberlain's Accounts for 1630 for 'Item for cariage of stone from the priory to ye scholehouse 3 shillings'.

What remained was the north aisle and nave of the Norman Priory Church, which at one time had been used as the Parish Church, the Parish Nave which had replaced the original South Aisle, and the new South Aisle and its porch. This left a nearly square building that was divided into three almost equal parts. The arcade between the Norman and Parish naves was soon blocked up and the Norman Nave used almost exclusively for burials. Vaults were created under the floor, the earth from which raised the floor level by some two feet, burying the bases and responds of the Norman columns (see the picture on the rear cover).

The next major event was a fire which was started on March 18th, 1699 by workmen repairing the roof. A contemporary account reveals the origin of this disaster:-

> The Church was covered with lead, laid upon a boarded roof. Between the board and the lead a quantity of peas-haulme [the stems and leaves of the pea plant] was laid, to bed the lead more evenly. The roof being out of repair, Mr. Tompkins, a plumber, was employed to repair the same. He and his men had been the morning part engaged, and had rolled up the lead, for the purpose of soldering the defected sheet. They had an iron pot with charcoal for heating their irons. They had left the Church to take their dinner, and the day being very blusterous, some sparks were blown into the peas-haulme, and set the whole on fire, which, melting the lead, rendered all assistance useless.

The result was the almost total destruction of the roof and much of the interior of the church.

The damage was such that the demolition of the ruins and the total rebuilding of the church were proposed, but once again the inhabitants of Leominster stepped in and subscribed the enormous sum of £16,500 to repair the existing structure. This included replacing the old arcade between the Parish Nave and the South Aisle with one using, rather incongruously, 'elegant Tuscan columns'. The building was reopened on May 26th, 1705.

Soon after this a Charity School was opened in Leominster, a schoolroom having been erected over the (fire) engine house adjoining the Forbury Chapel which was situated just north of the West Gate of the Priory. In order to accommodate the pupils for services in the church, a gallery was erected at the west end of the Parish Nave in 1722. This was enlarged in 1737 to accommodate the new organ. This inevitably damaged the Mowbray window.

In 1756 a further gallery was erected '... Against the North Wall and an arch sometime since filled up to extend when built from the East side of an Abuttment or Buttress of the said North Wall in length eighteen feet Eastward and in Breadth Southward from the said North Wall Seven feet ... Erect a Staircase in the North Isle [i.e. the Norman Nave] of the said Church and to make a doorway or passage under the said arch to the said Gallery.' This caused further damage to the Norman part of the fabric. The reason for this addition was given as the lack of seating space in the church due to the fact that private ownership of pews had become common and other people were not allowed to use them without an invitation from the owner. This new gallery was paid for privately and the five pews it contained remained in private ownership. A further private gallery was erected in the arch just east of the pulpit.

The porch was rebuilt in about 1800, the Rev. Jonathan Williams (headmaster of the Grammar School and author of *The Leominster Guide*, published in 1808) commenting that it had been done '... In a style of the most glaring incongruity, exhibiting, to the regret of every judicious spectator, a barbarous commixture of two orders of architecture the most opposite to each other.' It must be remembered, however, that the same gentleman described the Tuscan columns in the new arcade as 'elegant' and the Corinthian columns supporting the west gallery as 'handsome'.

In 1812 two of the ball-flower windows in the South Aisle, having fallen into complete disrepair, were replaced by two with simpler and undecorated tracery.

An even larger gallery was erected in the South Aisle in 1839-40, paid for by public subscription.

In May 1843 a Faculty was granted to erect a new gallery at the West End of the church, replacing the earlier ones, erect free seats in the centre aisle of the church, and 'to erect a stone

Interior of the Priory Church in 1860, showing the Parish Nave and South Aisle with some of the gallery pews to the right, and door to the vestry at the east end of the South Aisle. The free pews are ranged down the centre of the Parish Nave, with the organ in front of the east window

screen immediately at the back of the Communion Table at the Chancel or east end of the church and a Gallery or Loft behind the said Screen on which to place an organ'. The free seats, screen, gallery and organ are visible in a photograph of 1860 (above).

This was the last major change before Edward Freeman wrote his description and history of Leominster Priory Church for Rev. Townsend's book.

In a lecture on Leominster Priory Church given in Ludlow, Shropshire, in 1852 the historian Edward A. Freeman (1823-1892), who had published *A History of Architecture* in 1849, described the state of the church.

> The condition of the church might easily be improved. I am fully aware that perhaps no church in England must be more difficult to adapt to our present ritual; the old Norman nave and the southern additions are practically two distinct churches, utterly impossible to be employed by a single congregation; unless then, in so large a parish, they could anyhow be made available for distinct services, one portion must remain disused; this of course is the Norman nave, as the smaller of the two. This part therefore remains in that state of neglect and desolation which almost always seizes upon some portion of a parochialized minster, and which is even more unpleasant than one of total ruin. Still even its uncleanly whitewash is less offensive to the antiquarian eyes than the pewed, galleried, plastered and scored neatness of the adjoining portions, which has destroyed the evidence of masonry far more completely. Some of the

large windows seem in a dangerous state; and generally it would be desirable if the whole church could assume an uniform aspect which might be a sort of *tertium quid* between the dreariness of the one part and the spruceness of the other.

Sketches made c.1840 by W.H. Freeman showing the then state of the Norman part of the church

CHAPTER 2
A NEW BROOM – 1862

At the beginning of 1862 the vicar, Rev. G.F. Townsend, exchanged preferment with the Rev. Augustin Gaspard Edouart, then incumbent of St. Michael's Burleigh Street, Strand, London. St. Michael's, initially a chapel in the parish of St. Martin-in-the-Field's, was built in 1831-3 by the Church Building Commissioners and designed by James Savage in a style he called 14th-century Gothic. It was demolished in 1906. No explanation was given at the time as to why this exchange had been agreed but, in speeches given at the Church Soirée held in honour of Rev. Townsend, mention is made of the many difficulties he had had to contend with and one speaker commented 'I have observed his conduct in stormy times and in those of sunshine.' Part of the trouble would seem to have been due to a split in the Church of England in Leominster. The success of the missionary work by Mr. G. Onions, a lay preacher, later assisted by Thomas Smith, among the navvies building the railway, led to a mission room being built in Etnam Street in 1855 (now Leominster Museum). This movement received the support of two Hereford clergymen, especially Rev. John Venn. The mission seems to have also attracted a number of Rev. Townsend's congregation. Rev. Townsend also seems to have clashed with Mr. J. Southall, an eminent Quaker. It must be remembered that the then *Leominster News* was later owned and edited by members of the Southall family. However, in a letter dated February 6th, 1864 Townsend stated that 'The chief cause of my leaving the Parish was the failure in health of a very dear member of my family.' He went on to say 'I have had, as you know, many reasons for regretting my exchange from Leominster.' He had been in Leominster less than five years but he had found time to write a history of the town which had just been published.

The Rev. A.G. Edouart was born in London in 1817 but belonged to a well-known French family. His father, Augustin Amant Constant Fidèle Edouart, born in Dunkirk in 1783 and the sixteenth child of his parents, was a soldier under Napoleon. He distinguished himself in battle, was decorated for bravery, and was for a time Governor of Antwerp. Four of his brothers died on active service. He had married Emilie Vital and in 1814, the year in which Napoleon was banished to Elba, he found refuge, and a home in England. He had hoped to become a language teacher but there was too much competition and, for a time, he tried to earn his living by making portraits from hair, each hair being embedded in wax. He exhibited in the Royal Academy in 1815 and 1816 but it was not a financial success. The first of his five children, Augustin Gaspard, was born in 1817 and he subsequently had great difficulty in providing for his growing family. Then, to make matters worse, his wife died. A fortunate coincidence led to his discovering that he could make a living by cutting silhouettes with scissors. In this he was very successful and he is credited with having introduced the name 'Silhouette' to England. He travelled widely, first to Bath, Oxford, Cambridge and Cheltenham, and then to London and Edinburgh where his clients included Sir Walter Scott. There he was commanded to visit the palace of Holyrood and take profiles of the recently deposed King of France, Charles X, his Queen, the royal children and the entire suite. This unique collection is now in the Bibliothèque Nationale, Paris.

From Edinburgh he moved to Glasgow and Perth before going to Ireland where, after a year spent in Dublin, he travelled extensively. It was while he was in Ireland that he wrote *A Treatise on Silhouette Likenesses* which gives an insight into its author's life and adventures, as well as the subject of silhouettes.

In 1837-8 he toured British towns and then sailed from Liverpool to the USA where he remained until 1849, when he decided to retire and return to France. The *Oneida* on which he was travelling was wrecked in a storm on the coast of Guernsey. He and the other passengers escaped, but his carefully built up collection of copies of his work was mostly lost.

He seems to have been pompous and self-opinionated to a degree, a trait which he passed on to a certain extent to his eldest son, Gaspard. Gaspard, despite his Roman Catholic upbringing,

was attracted to the Church of England and was among the earliest students of King's College, London. He graduated at St. John's College, Cambridge with a B.A. in 1840, becoming a deacon the same year, and obtaining an M.A. in 1850. Curate of Deane in 1840-41 he was Ordained in 1841 by the Bishop of Chester, and was Perpetual Curate of St. Paul, Blackburn, from 1841-50 from where he moved to London. He was vicar of St. Michael's, Burleigh Street from 1850 to 1862, the year after his father's death.

During his stay at St. Michael's in London he was offered the bishopric of Sierra Leone, but had to decline it on the ground of his eyesight. He was interested in the work of the Society for Promoting the Employment of Additional Curates of which he was secretary from 1857 to 1859. He was known as a man of strong convictions, and one who was prepared to take independent action, if necessary, in the protection and defence of the rights and privileges of the clergy. He was inducted at Leominster by Rev. P. Hale of Burrington on February 15th, 1862 and preached himself in the following day.

The Rev. A.G. Edouart in later life (© The Dean and Chapter of Hereford and the Hereford Mappa Mundi Trust)

8

Fortunately Rev. Edouart's reactions to the state of the church as he found it on his arrival are on record in a report in the *Leominster News* for August 7th, 1885. The occasion was a public meeting under the presidency of the Lord Bishop of Hereford held in Leominster Town Hall to stimulate fund raising for what was by then the third phase of restoration.

Public worship was conducted in what was called the south church. The interior was rugged; there was a large three-decker pulpit of considerable height, with a sounding board above. There was a plaster ceiling and a large chandelier. The church had then galleries all round it, and was well stocked with very high pews, more like sheep pens than anything else. The Corporation seats were raised some three stairs. The Norman nave was in a state of great dilapidation. The floor was uneven, the ceiling partly decayed and the magnificent columns were buried 1½ feet in soil which had accumulated around them. Of course his [Gaspard's] first object was to go round and sound the people to see what could be done. It made his heart sick to see the state the church was in then. The pews — those great sheep pens — were all appropriated to different houses in the town, and there now hung in the vestry a list which those who felt interested in it might see, drawn up in the year 1705, showing who had the different pews.

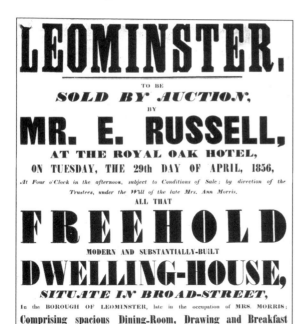

Sale notice of 1856 for a house in Broad Street which mentions 'An Excellent Pew in the Gallery of Leominster Church is attached to the House'

A photograph taken in about 1860 (see p.5) shows exactly what he was talking about.

He certainly lost no time before trying to do something about the appearance of the church for on Wednesday March 19th, just over a month after taking up his position, a Parish Meeting was held to consider the possibility of removing the organ. It was generally agreed that the organ in its position behind and above the altar was an eyesore. It was also agreed that the best place for it was in the vestry where the meeting was taking place. The vestry was under the gallery at the east end of the south aisle and the door to it can be seen in the 1860 photograph. Mr. William Gilkes, one of the Churchwardens, pointed out that this would require the removal of that part of the gallery and 'That could not be done, because the pews at the end of the gallery belonged to certain parties who were not likely to give them up.' He later commented that they '... could not suppose that a person who had paid £20 for a pew there would be inclined to give it up without some compensation or without having equally as good a place.'

In the seventeenth and eighteenth centuries the seating in the parish church reflected the rigid social structure. Rented accommodation varied from elaborate and ostentatious family pews to rectangular high-sided box pews which provided comparative privacy and comfort, and benches which were reserved for particular farms or tenements. There were both rented and freehold pews in Leominster Priory Church, along with a number of 'free' pews for visitors and the poorer parishioners (mainly the small pews that can be seen immediately in front of the altar). The freehold pews were attached to specific properties in the town as the sale notice for a property in Broad Street shows. This was actually one of the pews in the gallery erected on the north side of the parish nave in 1756 and can be seen in the bottom, left-hand corner of the 1860 photograph. The panelling that can be seen immediately below the 'roof' of the pulpit is the end of another small gallery. While providing a useful income for the church, these pews could lead to such behaviour as that described in the following account. 'I recollect being told by an aged lady visitor that, after waiting near a large empty pew, a young man came and unlocked it, locked himself in alone in the pew, put the key again into his waistcoat pocket, leaving her out in the cold!'. A suggestion that some of the 'free' seats be used to compensate for seats lost by the removal of part of the gallery caused the vicar to state '... the Church Building Society had made them a grant, on condition that there should be so many free seats in the Church; therefore those seats could not be converted into pews without making free seats elsewhere.' Mr. James then commented that he would oppose the curtailing of free seats '... which were the best occupied in the Church.' As a result of this discussion a further meeting was called for Tuesday May 13th, 1862 to discuss, among other things, the re-pewing of Leominster Church.

This meeting was not as well attended as the previous one, indeed a Mr. Coates (probably one of the shopkeepers of that name) commented 'Really, Mr. Chairman, I think part of the parish is asleep; they don't know anything of the meeting or of the purposes for which it is called. — Why three parts of the parish don't know that there is a parish meeting at this time,' but the Chairman (Rev. Edouart) protested that the proper notice had been posted up for two Sundays. Eventually a proposal was passed that a sum of over £1,500 be spent on re-pewing the church and various other items such as removing the organ and gas lighting, Mr. Coates being the sole dissenter.

However, Edwin Lloyd, a prominent lawyer in the town, made a very significant comment during his speech seconding the resolution proposed by Mr. William Gilkes, the senior churchwarden, a chemist and owner with his brother of Osborne mill where they produced printing ink and lamp black. Mr. Lloyd was of the opinion that they should look at the general state of the church, especially the walls, the ceilings, and the exterior of the windows and drew attention to the fact that several of the churches in the area such as Brecon, Ludlow and Hereford, had expended considerable sums on restoration. Both Brecon, which had been reopened in April 1862, and Hereford, where the restoration was ongoing, were under the charge of George Gilbert Scott.

Although the matter of general restoration was not debated at that meeting, Mr. Lloyd's comments had not fallen on deaf ears for in the two months that followed the Leominster Church Restoration Committee was set up. Mr. Nicholson, the Diocesan Architect, was called in to deliberate upon the removal of the organ, and he, together with Mr. Townsend Smith, the organist of Hereford Cathedral, made an inspection of the church, and submitted their ideas to the committee. On their suggestion a more extended scheme developed as a result of the interference with pew rights caused by the proposed removal of the organ to the east end of the South Aisle.

The committee were encouraged by the presence at the meeting of the Venerable the Archdeacon of Hereford who promised financial assistance. The committee then had a plan drawn up and estimates obtained for the entire re-fitting and re-flooring of the interior of the church, with other improvements. Just as they were about to advertise for tenders for carrying out these works, the ceiling of the Parish Nave, which had once or twice been patched up, coloured and repaired during the previous quarter century, was observed to have two or three large cracks through which drips of rain were falling onto the congregation below. As a result it was decided that a more extensive survey was needed to ascertain just what restoration was needed, and Mr. G.G. Scott was commissioned to make a report on the state of the church.

The composition of the Restoration Committee was significant. In addition to the clergy, who included the Venerable Archdeacon Lane Freer, D.D., there were three landowners: Elias Chadwick, Esq. of Puddlestone Court, Robert Lane, Esq. of Ryelands, a large house on the outskirts of Leominster, and John H. Arkwright, Esq., great-grandson of Sir Richard Arkwright of cotton fame, owner of Hampton Court, one of the biggest landowners in the county and Lord of the Manor of Leominster. Then there were three Magistrates and Aldermen of the Borough of Leominster: Thomas Burlton, Esq. a surgeon, T.B. Stallard, Esq., a Wine Merchant and soon to be the Mayor of Leominster, and James Bedford, Esq., an insurance agent and retired manager of the National Provincial Bank in Leominster. There were three lawyers: Thomas Sale, Esq., the Town Clerk, Henry Moore, Esq., Clerk to the Magistrates, and Edwin Lloyd, Esq., Treasurer to the Borough and, finally, there was Mr. H. Gamble, Clerk to the Union (Workhouse) and superintendent registrar, who acted as secretary.

Both Thomas Sale and Edwin Lloyd were frequently employed by Mr. Arkwright on legal matters and it seems to have been Mr. Arkwright who recommended (insisted on?) the employment of George Gilbert Scott who was still involved with the restoration of Hereford Cathedral. Mr. Arkwright's promise of £1,000 gave him a considerable say in how things were done, and ensured that the restoration commenced with the Norman Nave, while the vicar would have preferred to start with the Parish Nave. This matter remained a bone of contention between Rev. Edouart and Mr. Arkwright for the next thirty years.

The following circular letter was sent out in August, 1862:-

Address
The Leominster Church Restoration Committee

BEG to enclose a Report from Mr. G.G. Scott, on the Old Priory Church or Minster. To this Report they give their entire approval, and trust that the time has arrived, when, after a lapse of 800 years, that venerable edifice in which generations have worshipped, – and under the shadow of which they rest in hope, – may be restored to the full use for which it was erected, and to His Glory to whom it was first dedicated.

The Inhabitants as well as Land and Tithe Owners of the district of which Leominster is the centre, may fairly be expected to take an interest in the proposed undertaking, and the committee therefore hope that each, according to his means, will help to further a work, utterly beyond the power of the Parishioners to accomplish unaided.

Much of the proposed outlay, which it is estimated will be about £10,000, is, as will appear from Mr. Scott's Report, *absolutely necessary*. Accommodation for 1,800 persons will be provided by the alterations, and to many now compelled for want of room to seek religious instruction elsewhere, the opportunity will be afforded of offering up their prayers, and hearing the word of life in the Church of their Fathers.

If rich and poor would, for the time the work of Restoration is going on, *(a period of about five years),* devote a portion of their substance to this object, the whole of the proposed Restorations might easily be effected.

COMMITTEE
The Rev. Augustin G. Edouart, *Vicar*
Mr. William Gilkes, *Churchwarden*
Mr. H.N. Edwards, *Churchwarden*

John H. Arkwright, Esq.	Mr. Alderman Burlton
Elias Chadwick, Esq.	Mr. Alderman Stallard
Robert Lane, Esq.	Mr. Alderman Bedford
The Venerable Archdeacon Lane Freer, D.D.	
The Rev. J.F. Crouch, *Rural Dean*	
The Rev. G.T. Whitfield.	Thomas Sale, Esq.
The Rev. Edward C. Evans.	Henry Moore, Esq.
Capt. Turner	Edwin Lloyd, Esq.

The Committee earnestly solicit Contributions either by *Donations or Annual Subscriptions,* the extent of which may be notified upon the enclosed form, which may be forwarded to the Reverend the VICAR, or to Mr. H. GAMBLE, the Honorary Secretary.

Leominster, August 1ˢᵗ, 1862

To the Vicar, Churchwardens and the Committee for the Restoration of the Priory Church of Leominster.

GENTLEMEN: I have, as you requested, made a careful survey of your venerable Priory Church, with a view to forming an opinion as to its restoration.

Though it is needless for you, I will, to make my report intelligible to any one who may chance to read it, but is unacquainted with the church, commence with a hasty description of the general form, and the process by which it appears to have attained that form.

The church belonging to the Monastery, which dates from an early Anglo-Saxon period, was probable re-erected during the first half of the twelfth century, or possible in part during the later years of the eleventh. As was usual with great monastic churches it was a cruciform structure, with central tower; its choir was apsidal, with a continuous aisle or ambulatory round its eastern end, from which branched out three chapels – two nearly circular, and one (the eastern one) of an elongated form. From the eastern side of each transept also grew two apsidal chapels; the whole forming a perfect model of a monastic church of the Norman age.

It would appear that, as was so frequently the case, the nave was made use of as a parish church, but that during the thirteenth century the parochial and conventual authorities not agreeing, the former were distinctly provided for by the erection of a stupendous south aisle, or more properly a collateral nave, in the place of the low and narrow aisle of the old church. This aisle or second nave was of the same height and of about the same width with the original Norman nave, the triforium and clerestory of which are consequently enclosed within it.

Early in the fourteenth century, this second nave proving insufficient for the parish, a third was added, exactly equal in every way to the second, but a magnificent specimen of the altered style of this more advanced period. The western half of the church was thus made to consist of the following parts, a Norman nave, with its low massive pillars and arcades, its triforium and clerestory, on the north of this a low and narrow Norman aisle, and on the south of it a second nave in the early pointed, and a third nave in the decorated or middle pointed style, the earlier parts retaining their original form.

At the dissolution, however, the choir and transepts with the chapels and central tower were swept away, leaving the three naves and the one aisle, while, to compensate for the loss of the tower a smaller one was raised over the western bay of the Norman nave.

A century or two later the church was burnt, all the roofs and the arcade between the second and third naves being destroyed; and the church as barbarously restored after the calamity, and still further injured by pews, galleries; and the mutilations and decay of another century and a half, is what is come down to our day, and our task is to put this most interesting, though singularly irregular, mass of building into a seemly state, both as to reparation and with regard to its uses as a church.

FINALLY AS TO REPAIRS: The external stone work is in most parts very seriously decayed, and will require a general reparation. Several of the beautiful windows of the nave (some of the very noblest of their age) have been deprived of their tracery, and must be in a great measure repaired. The vast west window of the middle nave is in a most dangerous state, and must be almost wholly rebuilt. The pillars between the middle and south naves date from after the fire in 1690, and are a great disfigurement to the church. Their original form is ascertained from one of their capitals, which has been made use of in repairing the tower; and I would strongly recommend that they should be replaced by new ones of the original form. This would be a very great improvement, and would much reduce the obstruction which they at present cause from their undue size.

The stone work of the tower is especially bad in its condition, almost the entire surface having perished, and the walls become much shattered and disjointed, while the parapet and pinnacles (which seem to have been re-used from some earlier portions of the church) are in such a state of decay as to be extremely dangerous. The western end of the north aisle, the only part which retains its early vaulting is in a most shattered and dangerous condition, and the remainder of the aisle in a very mutilated and shabby state. The parapets generally demand considerable reparations; indeed, the repairs needed by the stone work, both within and without, are very heavy. I need hardly say that, internally, the stone work must be denuded of its thick coatings of whitewash, but without removing the ancient painting which in many parts exists below it, much less disturbing the ancient surface of the stone.

The roofs throughout are of a very miserable character, dating from after the fire.

The old nave is covered by a low lean-to roof which is far from strong. The middle nave has a roof of moderate pitch, and in itself substantial, but concealed by a wretched ceiling, parts of which threaten to fall upon the heads of those below. The third, or south, aisle has a lean-to roof tolerably though not substantially built, but unfit to be exposed, and concealed by a common plaster ceiling, and the roof of the old Norman nave is of a very rude and barn-like kind.

I do not like to recommend the re-construction of all these roofs, according to what may be supposed to have been their original forms, partly because of the great cost, and further, because the church having been reduced to a mere fragment of its original form, it is doubtful how far this might produce an agreeable effect. It is indeed clear that the older nave has not possessed a high pitched roof since the addition of the present tower. I further find that the timbers, uncouth though they are, are not much decayed, while the church having externally a sort of traditional aspect which is not unpleasing, I am rather unwilling to disturb it. I am for these reasons induced to recommend such internal modifications of the present roofs as may render them as sightly as may be, without going to the extend of re-constructing them.

The roof of the central nave can I think be, with a certain amount of modification, made to look very fairly well as an open roof. That of the south nave is much more difficult, but can, I think, be managed in a somewhat similar way, and strength added by the process. The roof of the old nave is still more difficult to deal with, and moreover needs very considerable additional strength. I am inclined to treat it as a level timber-framed ceiling, which I think is not unlikely to be nearly its original internal form, as Norman naves were usually covered with flat ceilings of timber decorated with colour below their high roof. One with another I think we can bring all the roofs internally into a sightly condition, and externally they require certain reparation of the lead-covering and gutters.

The ground immediately around the church ought to be lowered, so as to expose the original base-moulds, the foundations underpinned where required, and the drainage put into perfect order. The porch also demands general repairs and restoration.

I NOW COME TO THE INTERNAL FITTINGS : I will promise, for the information of any stranger into whose hands my report may chance to come, by saying, that though the demolishers of the monastic church spared the three naves and the one aisle, the more modern parishioners have apparently thought these remnants needlessly extensive, and have rejected the original nave and aisle, blocking them off from the remainder, and reducing the church practically to the two southern naves, which they have pewed and galleried up *ad libitum*.

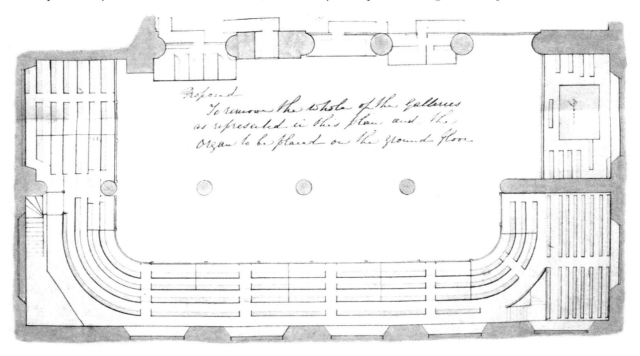

Scott's plan of the galleries as they existed at the time of his survey

14

Two things, then, are necessary as the first condition for bringing the interior into a seemly and consistent state for the uses of a large parish: firstly, to clear away all the modern pews and galleries, and, secondly, to open out the original nave and make full use of all which remains of the ancient church.

It is quite true that the church so opened out, will be one differing much from what one is in the habit of seeing, but this peculiarity is the great fact to which it will owe its interest, while the restoring to its sacred uses of the long disused Norman nave, will compensate for the loss of seats occasioned by the removal of the galleries, which at present obstruct and disfigure the two later naves.

A large portion of the north nave and its aisle will afford as good accommodation as that in the southern naves. This portion I would fit up with seats as the rest of the church, while the more distant parts may be furnished with chairs for more occasional use when the church is unusually full.

The church should be fitted up with good oak fittings, with new floors, and whatever else may be necessary to its completion.

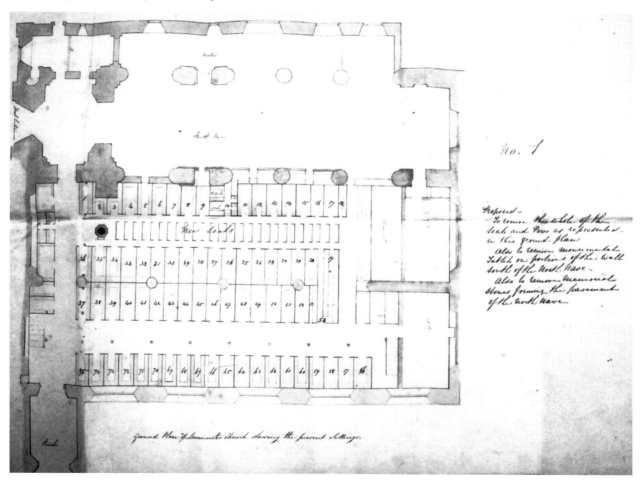

Scott's drawing of the floor plan in 1862

The cost of the above works I estimate as follows :-

	£
The repair of the South Nave and Porch	1700
' Middle Nave	1100
' North Nave and Aisle	1400
' Tower	900
New Floors, &c.	550
Drains and Ground Work	200
Re-fitting in Oak	2300
	£8150

Besides this, however, the lighting, warming, and other contingent expenses would have to be reckoned upon.

The above amount may appear startling at first sight, and I have given it in separate items, thinking it probable that the work may be more readily carried out in portions, and I can most heartily assure you, that for beauty and historical interest as well as for its peculiar and indeed unique characteristics, your church well deserves the thorough reparation which I have recommended, and which I am sure you have at heart to apply to it.

CHAPTER 3
GEORGE GILBERT SCOTT

George Gilbert Scott was born in 1811, his father being a low-church parson in north Buckinghamshire. He received no formal education, a fact of which he was very conscious throughout his life. He was given drawing lessons by a local master and some teaching in mathematics from his uncle who encouraged him to train as an architect. Joining up with W.B. Moffatt, who had trained with him, they worked hard and built up a busy practice. As an architect he designed everything from workhouses to the Foreign Office, from parish churches to the cathedral in St. John's Newfoundland, but it is for his restorations that he is best remembered. These included the whole range from the church at Upton Bishop to Canterbury Cathedral.

Despite, or perhaps because, of his success in the field of church restoration he had detractors in his own time, just as he has today. In the mid 19th century there were several schools of thought with regard to restoration. Firstly there were those who believed that anything was permitted to make a church suitable for use, including demolition and rebuilding. Scott commented that 'For years and years the vast majority of the churches to be restored have been committed to men, who neither know, nor care anything whatever about them, and out of whose hands they have emerged in a condition truly deplorable, stripped of almost everything which gave them interest or value; while it must be admitted that the best of us have been blameable, and that even our conservatism has been more or less destructive.'

The most vociferous were those who were against any form of restoration. The Anti-Restoration Movement was supported by John Ruskin who was a founder member of the Society for the Protection of Ancient Buildings and who, in 1874, declined the Gold medal of the Royal Institute of British Architects when Scott was President because he disapproved both of restoration and of professionalism. Referring to G.G. Scott in a letter to Thomas Carlyle, Ruskin was more explicit and implicitly critical of Scott: 'I cannot accept medals from people who let themselves out to build Gothic Advertisements for Railroads — Greek Advertisements for firms in the city — and — whatever Lord Palmerston or Mr. Gladstone chose to order opposite Whitehall — while they allow every beautiful building in France and Italy to be destroyed, for the 'job' of its restoration.'

Another critic was John James Stevenson (1832-1908) an architect born in Glasgow who had worked for Scott in London in the 1850s but soon took an adverse view of his restoration practice. He was another founder member of the Society for the Protection of Ancient Buildings. He attacked Scott in a paper on Architectural Restoration in 1877 to which Scott replied in a paper read at a meeting of the Institute of British Architects in May that year. After complaining of the misrepresentation of some of his work Scott made the following comment:

Sir George Gilbert Scott, by Charles Bell Birch
(courtesy of the National Portrait Gallery, NPG 2475)

The question, however, before us is not the truth of particular statements and criticisms (no doubt they are meant to be true, but things by superabundant zeal are seen through a distorting medium), but rather what is the true course to be followed? We are all agreed as to the calamity which the country has suffered [from bad restoration]; we differ as to the remedy. We do not differ widely as to the premises, though we may as to the conclusion to be drawn from them. Mr. Stevenson's view has an unquestionable *prima facie* advantage. It is certain that, if restoration were from this moment stopped, no new mischief would be done by it! Many persons have died from bad doctoring. If all medical treatment were prohibited, such disasters would unquestionably cease. Nor is this illustration imaginary, for a few years since a medical (or anti-medical) sect was founded, which ... styled itself the *'do nothing'* party. Their general acceptance would have done away for ever with deaths from overdosing, and who knows but that disease itself

would have fled before their frown? But the movement unfortunately failed, because misguided and impatient patients would not be persuaded to allow themselves to be let alone.

Later in the same paper Scott lists four suggestions as to the most useful fields to which the Society for the Protection of Ancient Monuments should direct their exertions and follows them with some remarks on the restoration of churches.

1. To press upon the proprietors of ruined buildings the duty of protecting them as much as possible from increasing decay by securing the tops of the shattered walls from wet.

2. To find out and oppose, while there is time, the contemplated destruction of ancient buildings, down even to those of the last century. The losses we are constantly sustaining by the actual destruction of old buildings are truly appalling! Of timber buildings, which are constantly being taken down as ruinous, I assert that timely and judicious reparation is the only possible means for their preservation.

3. To have measured drawings made, systematically and constantly, of all the unprotected architectural antiquities of our land, that when, in the course of nature, their architecture perishes, authentic drawings may remain behind.

4. I am ready and willing to take my share, where I deserve it, in the protests against bad restoration, but I beg the Society to recollect that the great majority of ancient buildings are committed to the mercy of a herd who trample them under their feet and turn again and rend all objectors. Let this herd at least have a share of censure, or their patrons will conclude that they have done rightly in casting their pearls before them.

Scott's signature

Scott was very aware that the churches he restored were for every-day religious use and that allowance had to be made for changes in ritual, as well as the personal tastes and prejudices of the people who were his employers. The restored church had to be fit for modern ecclesiastical use. Scott's comments about pewing are particularly pertinent in the case of Leominster Priory Church, especially the lack of 'free' pews which, he said had 'driven God's poor from their own churches'.

Mr. Stevenson talks of the 'dreary ranges of low benches,' and truly they do often look dreary enough, but I do not know that they are more so than high pews which half bury the pillars. Let us not, however, judge of churches only when empty: 'empty benches' are proverbially dreary: let us rather see them when thronged by devout worshippers, and the dreariness of the seat-backs will not much trouble either eye or memory. Better see the people than have them buried to the neck in Georgian 'dozing pens.' Let the Society make up their minds at once that any attempt to banish religious motives from the treatment of churches is suicidal; and let them rather aim — this being taken for granted — at making us do this necessary and religious work with the smallest possible sacrifice of history and antiquity.

Scott took on amazing amount of work but he would seem to have preferred smaller projects in areas where he already had major ones. Herefordshire is a good example, the following being a list of contracts:

1852	Eastnor, St. John. Designed by Scott with the exception of the 14th-century west tower
1856/7	Tedstone Delamere, St. James. Chancel added.
1860	Edvin Loach, St. Mary. New church designed by Scott.
1862	Upton Bishop, St. John Baptist. Restoration.
1863	Aconbury, St. John Baptist. Restoration.
1864	Yarpole, St. Leonard. Chancel rebuilt and new north aisle added.
1868	Cradley, St. James. Chancel added.

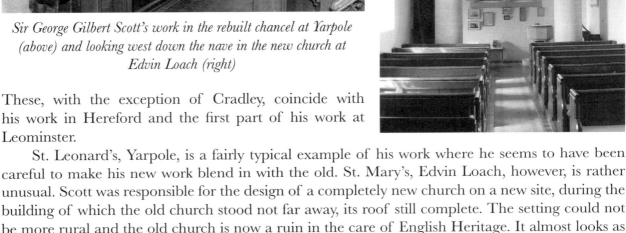

Sir George Gilbert Scott's work in the rebuilt chancel at Yarpole (above) and looking west down the nave in the new church at Edvin Loach (right)

These, with the exception of Cradley, coincide with his work in Hereford and the first part of his work at Leominster.

St. Leonard's, Yarpole, is a fairly typical example of his work where he seems to have been careful to make his new work blend in with the old. St. Mary's, Edvin Loach, however, is rather unusual. Scott was responsible for the design of a completely new church on a new site, during the building of which the old church stood not far away, its roof still complete. The setting could not be more rural and the old church is now a ruin in the care of English Heritage. It almost looks as though Scott had joined the 'do noting' brigade, although there seem to have been reasons behind the decision not to restore the old church.

CHAPTER 4
GETTING STARTED — THE NORMAN NAVE: 1863–1866

Mr. Edward Freeman gave a lecture on 'The Priory Church of Leominster.' in Leominster Town Hall on December 9th, 1862, thus helping to arouse further interest in the project. Freeman and Scott had been friends for some time, in fact they had corresponded from as far back as 1846 and there is correspondence concerning Leominster Priory Church in 1864.

The first step the restoration committee had to take was to get permission for the work to be done. An application was made to the Consistory Court in Hereford which then invited parishioners to show cause against the Grant of a Licence to remove the pews. Thomas Brayen, a farmer who lived in South Street and was a member of the Town Council was one who objected and had to identify his pew. He stated 'that in or about the year of our Lord 1705 a certain seat or pew then occupied by one James Caswell and his Tenants and situate on the South side of the said Parish Church of Leominster having a Seat wherein Thomas Rawlings Thomas Badgnedge and others then usually sat on the East and a Seat wherein Thomas Vale and others then usually sat on the West and the Alley of the said Church on the North parts thereof containing in length 9 feet and 2 inches and in breadth 4 feet and 5 inches and a half was by the then Minister and Churchwardens of the said Parish appointed and allotted to three several houses in the town of Leominster aforesaid, etc. etc.'

Each of these claims had to be verified and an accommodation reached, allocating the people concerned spaces in the new layout. The Court granted a Faculty dated August 13th, 1863, part of which is quoted below. It is interesting to note just how much of it concerned the pews.

TRAVERS TWISS Doctor of Civil Law Vicar general and Official Principal of the Right Reverend Renn Dickson by Divine permission Lord Bishop of Hereford Lawfully Constituted. ***To all whom these Presents shall come*** or whom the same shall or may in any wise concern ***Greeting Whereas*** **it** hath been alleged before us on the part of the Reverend Augustin Gaspard Edouart Clerk Vicar of the Vicarage and Parish Church of Leominster in the county and diocese of Hereford and William Gilkes and Henry Nicholas Edwards the Churchwardens of the said Parish that they are desirous of removing the whole of the present and existing Seats and Pews in the Parish Church of Leominster aforesaid and of replacing the same with new and more commodious and open Seats and Pews suitable to the present requirements of the said Parish And that they are also desirous of taking up the present Floors in the said Church and of laying down new Floors therein And that they are also desirous of taking off the crown of the Arch of certain Vaults in the North Nave in order to enable them to bring the Floor of such Nave to its original level (the same being now from eighteen inches to two feet higher than when originally formed) and of lowering such Vaults and replacing and fixing the Crown of the Arch of such Vaults so interfered with below the surface of the floor when so lowered and of covering the ground immediately beneath the floor of the said Nave with a layer of concrete And that they are also desirous of removing the monumental Tablets on portions of the Wall south of the North Nave of the said Church and of placing and fixing the Organ (which now stands in one of such Galleries) on the ground Floor of the said Church according to the plans numbered 1, 2, and 3 and Specification which have been laid before and approved by us **And Whereas** on the seventh day of January last a certain Citation with Intimation was issued out of and under the seal of our Consistory Court of Hereford citing the parishioners Landholders Householders and Inhabitants of the said Parish of Leominster in special and all others in general having or pretending to have any right title or interest in the premises aforesaid to appear before us our lawful Surrogate or other competent judge in this behalf at the College of the Cathedral Church of Hereford and in our Consistory place of Judicature there or in such other place as our said Court should then be sitting on Thursday the fifteenth day of January last between the hours of nine and twelve of the clock in the forenoon of the same day or as soon as our said Court should then and there be sitting and then and there to shew cause if any they had or knew why a Licence or Faculty should not be granted to the said Augustin Gaspard Edouart Clerk William Gilkes and Henry Nicholas Edwards our Licence or Faculty for the purposes aforesaid **And Whereas** the said Citation with Intimation was duly published by publicly affixing the same with a true Copy thereof on a conspicuous part of the principal outer Door of the said Parish Church of Leominster previous to the commencement of Diving Service on Sunday the eleventh day of January last and by leaving the same original Citation with Intimation and also the said true Copy thereof so affixed during the whole time of Diving Service in the said parish Church in the morning of the said Sunday the eleventh day of January last and by afterwards leaving the said true Copy of the said original Citation with Intimation affixed to the said Church Door as appears by the Certificate of Thomas Pitchford was duly sworn on the said fifteenth day of January last **And Whereas** upon the return of the said Citation into Court divers persons being Householders and Parishioners of the said Parish of Leominster claiming certain Seats or pews in the said Parish Church by virtue of certain Faculties formerly granted by our said Consistory Court appeared and opposed the grant of such Faculty in respect of which the several Faculties mentioned and set forth in the fourth Column of the same Schedule were respectively granted have by several proxies under their respective hands and Seals and filed and now remaining in the Registry of our said Court and through the intervention of their Proctor respectively consented to the removal of the whole of the present and existing Seats and pews in the said Schedule be granted and confirmed to them for the use of the occupiers and inhabitants of their respective Messuages or Tenements in lieu of the Seats or pews granted by their said respective Faculties **And Whereas** Charles Hughes of the parish of Eardisland etc. etc.

The Faculty includes a plan of the proposed new layout and a Schedule showing, among many others that Thomas Brayen (mentioned above), who owned a property in Etnam Street and had been granted a Faculty for a pew or seat in the year 1640 was allocated seat or pew numbered 20 in the new plan, James Harris and Elizabeth Wilkes who owned two properties in Etnam Street the original Faculty for which was granted on September 11th, 1753, now had pew 39, etc.

The receipt of this Faculty and the money being collected or promised meant that work could begin. It was not long before it was discovered that there was more that needed doing than had appeared at first. It had been realized that the north wall needed underpinning for it was beginning to lean outwards, but the pressure being exerted by the tower led Scott to build a buttress between the two blocked windows that he had opened up. The North Aisle was extended by the addition of a window at the east end matching the other two and timbers inserted to support the new roof and the level, timber-framed, ceiling which was decorated by Messrs. Clayton and Bell of London. But on the south side of the Norman Nave the removal of the crude walls that had filled in the Norman arches of the arcade, and the lowering of the floor to reveal bottom of the pillars showed that they had been more damaged by the fire of 1699 than had been thought. After the roof had collapsed the debris continued to burn, shattering some of the stone at the base of the columns. Add this to the damage caused by some of the mural tablets and the erection of the galleries, with their associated staircases, on the other side of the wall, and the whole of the arcade had to be underpinned as well as restored, the arches having to be shored up while the work was in progress.

The floor presented problems owing to the burial vaults built underneath (probably in the 18th century) as the crowns of the arches of these were higher than the original floor level. Permission had been granted to remove the crown of these arches and the whole floor was sealed by a layer of concrete. The floor was then covered by encaustic tiles in red and black made by Godwins of Lugwardine.

Part of Scott's sketch of the rmeains of the Wheel of Life discovered on west end of the north aisle

It is probable that Scott, who had mentioned paintings in his report, repeated the instructions he had issued in Hereford a few years before, that the 'uncleanly' whitewash described by Mr. Freeman was to be removed by chemical means. He also stressed that if any wall paintings were found, these were to be inspected by the architect. The work was commenced and, sure enough, wall paintings were found. Unfortunately the workmen started to remove the plaster on which they were painted. When Scott heard of this he called an immediate halt to the work and appointed Mr. Chick, a Hereford architect, to act as clerk of works, having held a similar post under Mr. Scott at Hereford Cathedral. There seems to be no record of the paintings that were destroyed, but fortunately he took the necessary action in time to preserve the Wheel of Life that was discovered on the wall at the west end of the north aisle. Another Wheel of

Life was discovered in 1872 painted on the wall of St. Mary's Church, Kempley, but they were, and remain, extremely rare subjects for church decoration. Most of the known examples are on the continent in Chartres, etc., but there is an excellent example in the Arundel Psalter in the British Museum. The painting is now faint and, because of its position behind a window over the choir vestry, difficult to see, but it was copied by Mr. C.J. Praetorius, a Fellow of the Society of Antiquaries and published in their *Proceedings* for January, 1914, in an excellent paper by G. McN. Rushforth, Esq. on the 'Wheel of the Ten Ages of Life in Leominster Church'. Scott found this painting interesting and his sketchbook contains two pages of sketches which are reproduced here.

This end of the North Aisle had once been the Chapel of St. Anthony and was the only part which retained its early vaulting, but it was in such a dangerous condition as to require almost complete reconstruction. It was converted by Scott into a baptistery, and the font, which was the

Mr. J.C. Praetorius' drawing of the Wheel of Life at Leominster and published in 1914

gift of Canon Evans, and was a copy of that in Magdalen Hall, Oxford, was removed from the Parish Nave and placed on a stone platform. There is a room over this chapel, lit by a circular window, which had been sealed with masonry when the monastery was suppressed. On being opened the floor was found to be sprinkled with cuttings of human hair with a noticeable red tinge, giving rise to the supposition that this had been the monks' barber's shop.

The external stonework of the north wall was repaired where necessary and the wall raised to clear the window heads and provide support for the new roof.

The east end of the nave was temporarily fitted up as a chancel with a raised platform. The old pulpit was cut down and placed on a lower base, seats placed for the choir and the remainder of the nave furnished with chairs for the use of the congregation. Temporary gas fittings were installed.

The contractor was a Mr. Coleman of Chasehill, Westbury-on-Severn, near Gloucester.

As the head of the busiest architectural practice in the country Scott was involved in many other projects at this time. They included the restoration of Yarpole Church completed in 1864, with the addition of a new North Aisle (see also pp.19-20).

Norman Nave looking E., Priory Church, Leominster.

A photograph of c.1870 showing the restored Norman Nave

The north side of the church c. 1866-1890

The work at Leominster was completed by June, 1866 and Saturday, June 30th was fixed for the re-opening ceremony. The re-opening services commenced with the celebration of Holy Communion at eight o'clock, followed by divine service in the newly restored nave at eleven. The second lesson was read by Rev. Sir Henry Williams Baker, the vicar of Monkland, who was an editor of and contributor to *Hymns Ancient and Modern* which had been published the year before. He had taken a great interest in the restoration and was an honorary member of the restoration committee.

The sermon was preached by the Ven. Archdeacon of Hereford, Lord Saye and Sele, who had also taken a practical interest in the restoration. Among his comments on the work carried out was a reference to 'the plague spot of British churches — their thick coats of white and brown plaster'. His lordship was full of praise for Scott's work, although he drew attention to the fact that the actual cost of this portion of the work had largely exceeded the estimate given in the architect's report. George Gilbert Scott had estimated the cost of the whole restoration to be approximately £10,000, and the cost of restoring the Norman Nave alone was £3,017 11s. 6d. The collection after the service realized the sum of £37 4s. 2d.

The only adverse comment about the service concerned the accompanist and that was put down to a lack of practice and the fact that a harmonium was used, the organ still being in the Parish Nave.

The service was followed by a luncheon in the Town Hall provided by Mr. Weaver, confectioner, of Church Street but concerning which some diners complained at the cost of the tickets.

No mention was made in the reports of John Hungerford Arkwright, Esq. his absence being possibly explained by his marriage to Miss Charlotte Lucy Davenport, of Foxley on the 12th of the same month. The return from their honeymoon was delayed until July 3rd owing to the bride's indisposition.

CHAPTER 5
TO BE CONTINUED: 1866–1875

Work seems to have started right away on the rest of the church, for this was the main target of Rev. Edouart's plans for restoration. His agreement for the work to begin with the north aisle and Norman Nave seems to have been rather reluctant, his preferences having been overruled by both G.G. Scott and John Hungerford Arkwright so, to quote Scott, 'As a preparation for further restoration, the incongruous arrangement of pews and Galleries has been swept away from the South [Parish] Nave and its Aisle, and the Northern nave and North Aisle have been furnished with temporary fittings'. The organ was moved from its perch behind the altar and placed in the north aisle. Unfortunately, when this had been done, the money seems to have run out, for work was stopped, not to recommence until 1876.

In an attempt to explain this sudden hiatus in the subscription of funds for the restoration I looked at some causes of friction between the Vicar and his parishioners. As later correspondence shows, there was a difference of opinion between Rev. Edouart and J.H. Arkwright, Esq., but it uncertain at what date this difference began, and how much it affected the work of the Restoration Committee of which Mr. Arkwright was a prominent member. However, there were at least two occurrences that upset the even tenor of life within the Church.

The first was the curious matter of the choir, did it resign or was it sacked? What seems to have happened is that there was a falling out between the Vicar and the choir and organist. The reasons for this are a bit obscure, depending on whose version of events you believe, but the choir claimed that the Vicar insisted on their meeting for practice on Wednesday evenings, a night on which they could not attend because of a 'class meeting'. The Vicar had previously remarked that those who could not

The organ in the North Aisle in the 1870s

attend practices should be 'culled out'. There was correspondence published in the *Hereford Times* in July, 1863, the members of the choir finally signing themselves as 'The Late Members of the Leominster Church Choir'. The congregation left little doubt about their opinion of the matter when the following report appeared in the *Hereford Times* for September 8th, 1863:

> PRESENTATION On Thursday a presentation of a most gratifying and pleasing nature was made to the gentlemen lately forming the Church Choir, the present consisting of a handsomely bound copy of 'Hymns, Ancient and Modern' in acknowledgment of long and past services. To Mr. Wood, the conductor, was also given a purse containing eight guineas. The following presentation address, neatly printed in gold, with the name written, was inserted in each book:— 'Presented to the gentlemen lately forming the choir of the parish church of Leominster, by the Congregation, in appreciation of several years' voluntary services efficiently and cheerfully given by them. 1863'.

The second matter was more serious and concerned the Curate, the Rev. Hugh Reed. His entry in Crockford's *Clerical Directory* for 1865 reads:

> REED, Hugh, *Leominster*.— Deacon 1836 and Priested 1837 by Bishop of Jamaica. Curate of Leominster 1862. Formerly Incumbent of Vere, Jamaica, 1836; Chaplain to Royal Artillery and Naval and Military Hospital 1838; Incumbent of Lemi Savanna, Jamaica, 1845; Curate of St. Sepulchre's, London 1859.

In a pamphlet published by Rev. Reed in 1858 he claimed to be the Officiating Minister at St. Martin-in-the-Fields, London, virtually around the corner from Rev. Edouart's church in Burleigh Street, Strand. The title-page of this pamphlet read as follows:-

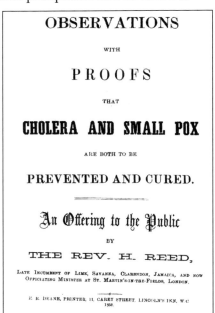

In the *British Medical Journal* published on October 5th, 1862 the following appeared under the heading Herefordshire Medical Association: 'That this Association strongly disapprove of medical men publishing scales of charges, or otherwise advertising for practice, the more particularly so, when done for private motives under the guise of charity.' Messrs. James and Boyce from Leominster, having laid before the meeting a statement regarding the conduct of the curate of that town in practicing medicine to the injury of the public, it was proposed and seconded, 'That the Committee collect information regarding the irregular proceedings of the Rev. Hugh Reed at Leominster, and adopt such a course in reference thereto as may appear most desirable.' The core of the complaint was 'His use of a secret remedy for his own profit.'

At a meeting of the Leominster Curate's Fund Committee held at Leominster Town Hall on December 14th, 1863, the whole matter of his medical pretensions was discussed and the following resolution was passed:

RESOLVED—
That the Members of the 'Leominster Curate Fund Committee,' present at the Meeting, whilst recognizing the necessity for the employment of an efficient Curate for the Vicar's assistance, and for the good of the people generally in the extensive parish of Leominster, do respectfully express their opinion, that the REV. HUGH REED, the present Curate, has forfeited all claim to their support that therefore no further Subscriptions should be given to meet the grant of the 'Curates' Aid Society,' for payment of the stipend of the said REV. HUGH REED, as such Curate; and that a copy of this resolution be sent to, and notice given to the Rev. The Vicar of Leominster, that this Committee will not be answerable for the stipend payable to the said REV. HUGH REED further than up to the 24th of June, 1864.

The Committee's objection was not just that he was claiming to cure cancer by methods he was unwilling to divulge to the medical profession, but also that he was charging up to 'a hundred guineas to be paid in weekly instalments of twenty-five guineas from the commencement of the treatment, the last instalment only to be left till the completion of the cure'. This and other information was published in a 36-page pamphlet in December 1862 entitled:

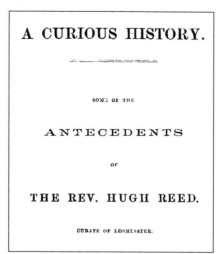

It consisted mainly of extracts from *'Cancer Cures and Cancer Curers'* by T. Spencer Wells, F.R.C.S. which included a long section on the Rev. Hugh Reed as well as several excerpts from the *Medical Times & Gazette* for various dates in 1860. One of these excerpts contains a letter from

Rev. Edouart, then resident at St. Michael's Parsonage, Burleigh Street, Strand, to Rev. Hugh Reed which had been produced by Rev. Reed to support one of his claims for a cancer cure. This led to the publication of five further pamphlets, the last dated March 1st, 1864, their titles being as follows:-

January 1864:

WHEN IS A COMMITTEE NOT A COMMITTEE ?

WHEN IT WOULD BE A BISHOP.

AN ENIGMA,

CUDGELLED, GUESSED, AND DISPOSED OF

BY HUGH REED,

CURATE OF LEOMINSTER.

LEOMINSTER:
PRINTED BY JOHN WOOLLEY, POST OFFICE, BROAD STREET.
MDCCCLXIV.

January 20th, 1864:

A HISS FOR A QUACK!

OR,

SOMETHING TO READ!

BEING A

CRITIQUE UPON THE PAMPHLET

OF

"HUGH REED, CURATE OF LEOMINSTER."

BY QUIS ?

"History tells
How Rome escaped the Gauls,
Thanks to a timely Goose that hissed
From Capitolian walls."

"Sint sales sine vilitate."

"Ecclesiæ magis favendum est quam personæ."

LEOMINSTER:
PRINTED BY S. PARTRIDGE, BOOKSELLER, BROAD STREET.

January 30th, 1864:

"The Truth, the Whole Truth, and Nothing but the Truth."

A

PLAIN STATEMENT OF A FEW SIMPLE FACTS,

OR

SOMETHING TO REFLECT UPON,

IN ANSWER TO

"QUIS."

BY

REV. A. G. EDOUART, M.A.,

(ST. JOHN'S COLLEGE, CAMBRIDGE)

VICAR OF LEOMINSTER.

LEOMINSTER:
PRINTED AND PUBLISHED BY MRS. J. WENT, SOUTH STREET.

February 8th, 1864:

LEOMINSTER VINDICATED!

OR;

"THE TRUTH, THE WHOLE TRUTH, AND NOTHING BUT THE TRUTH," AS COMING FROM THE REV. A. G. EDOUART:

REVIEWED, REVISED, & CORRECTED

BY QUIS ?

WITH HIS REFLECTIONS THEREUPON.

LEOMINSTER:
PRINTED BY S. PARTRIDGE, BROAD STREET.

March 1st, 1864:

THE GLASS HOUSE:

OR A REFLECTION OF

"THE TRUTH, THE WHOLE TRUTH, AND NOTHING BUT THE TRUTH."

BY ALIQUIS.

SECOND EDITION.

LEOMINSTER:
PRINTED BY S. PARTRIDGE, BROAD STREET.

The use of *noms de plume* was quite normal at that time; even the most innocuous letter to the newspapers could be signed with one.

The Curate's Fund was established between 1853 and 1857, while Mr. Westmorland was Vicar of Leominster, in connection with the Pastoral Aid Society. When Mr. Townsend was appointed, the Curate's Aid Society promised an annual grant of £40 on condition that a similar sum was obtained from other sources. This was later increased to £60. The annual payment of these sums was guaranteed by a committee of which Mr. James Bedford was appointed Treasurer.

It is pointless to go over all the endless arguments in these pamphlets and elsewhere, but one point is important. Rev. Edouart supported his Curate in the argument even when Mr. Reed accused Mr. Bedford of lying. Now Mr. James Bedford was an important and well respected figure in Leominster. He was an Alderman and had been Mayor of Leominster in 1854 and 1855 as well as a Magistrate and Manager of the National Provincial Bank. He was also a leading member of the Church Restoration Committee, not the sort of person to be antagonized when the restoration fund was short of cash.

The affair came to a rather curious end. The last pamphlet was published on March 1st, 1864. Rev. Edouart had implied that he had the full support of the Bishop of Hereford but it would appear that the Bishop was not very happy with the situation. He seems to have looked into the Rev. Reed's antecedents and come up with an unexpected solution. On August 15th of the same year the following citation was served personally to Rev. Hugh Reed:

> Renn Dickson by Divine permission Lord Bishop of Hereford To the Reverend Hugh Reed Clerk officiating as Curate in the Parish Church of Leominster etc. etc. **Whereas** it has been represented to us that you the said Hugh Reed have been admitted to Holy Orders by a Bishop other than those of England and Ireland and that you are officiating in the said Parish Church of Leominster aforesaid without Special permission from the Most Reverend the Lord Archbishop of Canterbury and acting as Curate therein without consent and approbation of the Most Reverend Lord Archbishop contrary to the provisions of a statute passed in the fifty ninth year of his late Majesty King George III entitled 'An Act to permit the Archbishops of Canterbury and York and the Bishop of London for the time being to admit persons into Holy orders specially for the Colonies.' **And whereas** under the provisions of the said Statute you are incapable of so officiating without the special permission of the said Most Reverend Lord Archbishop and your appointment to act as such Curate being contrary to the provisions of the said Statute is null and void. **We hereby** Cite you to appear before us in the Great Hall of our Palace situate in the City of Hereford on the twenty seventh day of August instant at the hour of twelve o'clock of the same day to show cause why the said Licence granted to you by us should not be revoked by us and to do and receive as unto law and justice shall appertain under law and contempt thereof.

The Rev. Reed duly appeared and gave his reasons in writing why he thought his Licence should not be revoked. The Bishop's verdict was served on September 9th, 1864 saying that 'We do from the day and date of these presents revoke annul and make void the said licence so granted by us to you as Stipendiary Curate of the Parish Church of Leominster.' Reed appealed to the Archbishop of Canterbury, probably with the backing of Rev. Edouart, and on March 4th, 1865 the Archbishop wrote annulling the Revocation of the Curate's Licence. However the Rev. Hugh Reed disappeared from the scene.

The pewing arrangements of 1866 in the Norman Nave did not meet with universal approval. Alderman James complained that the two small pews allotted to the Corporation 'would inconveniently accommodate ten persons only'. The matter was settled amicably when the churchwardens and the Alderman moved a vote of thanks to them for their prompt action. Unfortunately the vicar preached a sermon in which they were told 'that they wanted the highest places in the synagogue, and would be content with none but high backed cushioned seats.' Alderman James took exception to this but said that the vicar's sarcasm, 'like water poured on a duck's back, rolled away without doing injury'. However it did nothing to improve relations between the vicar and some of the leading citizens of the town.

Mr. Jones' photographs of the Parish nave from the east (above) and South Aisle from the west (below) prior to their restoration

The Parish Nave and South Aisle stayed as shown in the two photographs by Mr. Jones alongside, but in 1875 a new Leominster Church Restoration Committee was formed. With Rev. A.G. Edouart as chairman it comprised Charles Davis Andrews, a solicitor; Thomas Bannister, a clothier, hatter, and general outfitter, as well as Registrar for Marriages and Deputy Registrar for Births and Deaths; William Daggs, a magistrate and manager of the Leominster Branch of the Worcester City and County Bank (later taken over by Lloyds); Thomas Graves, linen and woollen draper; James Harding, draper; Theophilus William Lane, M.A., J.P., D.L. of the Ryelands, landowner; Edwin Lloyd, solicitor and the only surviving member of the original Restoration Committee; John Manwaring, of South Villa, Hereford road; Thomas Toogood, grocer, of Westgate House; Thomas Bristow Stallard, a wine merchant; and John Woolley, postmaster, book seller, stationer and printer.

CHAPTER 6
A FRESH START: 1875

The first step this committee took was to commission a new report on the state of the church. Scott had been knighted in 1872, largely because of his work on the Albert Memorial, so it was Sir George Gilbert Scott they now employed to compile the new report. After a brief summary of the work that had already been completed and the preparations made for the second stage of the restoration he reported as follows:-

> The works now remaining to be done are of no small extent. They comprise the complete external and internal restoration and refitting of the South Nave and its Aisle, the repairs of the Porch and Tower, together with some external restoration of the Nave and North Aisle, which were postponed for want of funds when the former restoration was carried out. In addition to these essential works the extension of the South or Main Nave, in the form of an Apse as has been suggested by your Bishop, seems very desirable to give a Chancel like arrangement to the interior.
>
> In my former Report I directed attention to the very serious condition of much of the Stonework, and the lapse of thirteen years has greatly increased the extent of the dilapidations. The great Western window of the Nave is in imminent danger of falling, and the tower parapet has been so weakened by decay that one side has actually been blown down and a second side has had to be removed to avoid a like fate. The mullions and tracery of the windows of the Aisle are so insecure that their fall may happen at any time. These instances are sufficient to shew that the restoration now contemplated is most urgent.
>
> Besides the very serious defects just stated, the stonework of the exterior needs general reparation. The ground which is much above the level of the floor inside should be removed from the base of the walls, the foundations where necessary underpinned and a general system of drainage carried out. The respond of the Arch of the Central tower at the South East Angle of the Norman Nave needs partial rebuilding; in consequence of its failure the abutting arch and wall on the inside have become rent. This rent will require to be carefully bonded across. The Porch which is partially buried needs to have its archway opened down to its former level, and the outer mouldings which have been barbarously cut away, restored. The plastered ceiling should be replaced by a substantial oak roof.
>
> The treatment of the interior of the South Nave and Aisle, at first presents some difficulty as we have no evidence of the original designs of the Arcade and Roofs; and those which we now find are so fairly substantial that their entire rejection would seem to involve a needless expense.

I therefore propose to adapt what we find, making it as consistent as possible with the general character of the later portion of the building, without professing to view these features as a restoration in the proper sense of the word.

The Arcade I would improve in appearance by supplying new piers of less height and diameter and of more graceful form than the present, sustaining but slightly altering in form the superincumbent Arches. The roofs are of oak in tolerably good condition, these I would repair and strengthen, and add panelled and moulded ceilings in oak below the main constructive timbers.

The level of the floor of this portion of the Church is, and has been at least from the 14th century, higher than that of the Norman Nave. The higher level will have to be approached by steps from the lower floor, but this difference practically will be of little or no inconvenience as the Main Nave with its Aisle will afford accommodation for the bulk of the Congregation within sight of the Chancel and pulpit. The most suitable part of the Norman Nave may be seated for constant use, and for exceptional occasions the remaining spaces may be filled with chairs. The eastern part of the South or Main Nave I propose to form into a quasi-chancel fitted with stalls, and have adopted in my plan the Bishop's proposal to throw out an Apse to form the Sanctuary or Altar space. The Arcade I continue one bay eastward piercing by an additional Arch the present blank wall, so as to allow the Chancel to be seen from the Eastward part of the South Aisle. The Organ would be well placed against the blank part of the Eastern wall of the Aisle, the pipes might rise on either side of the window if necessary. The Organist would see and be sufficiently near the Choir. The whole of this arrangement would I think be found to be satisfactory in appearance and in use.

The lead covering the roof of the South Nave and Aisle is very defective, this should be taken off recast and re-laid on new boarding. The interior of the walls will need considerable cleansing and repair and the windows must be reglazed. The floor should be lowered to its original level and have the pavement and wooden flooring laid down. New doors to the Porch will be necessary.

The seats and other fittings might be left until the substantial repairs to this part of the Church and the Tower have been done.

A receptacle for fuel &c. may be provided by enclosing the space at the east end of the South Aisle next the Apse.

The Tower from the level of the Nave roof upwards is in a most deplorable condition nearly the whole of the surface being so far decayed, that little short of the entire renewal of the external Stonework will be necessary. The buttresses instead of giving support to the tower are themselves falling away and only held in place by iron cramps. The weather now finds its way into porous stones and open joints, and every frost causes the dislodgement of flakes of stone. The parapet as I have before mentioned is partly displaced, the whole of it should be renewed in the same form as before, but strengthened by piers on the inside. The pinnacles besides repair, need completion by the addition of proper finials. The Tower is rent in several places by settlement and should be well bonded together by iron ties or strong stones built across the rents. The roof requires releading.

The Norman Nave and North Aisle although repaired internally require some external repairs and pointing. The Nave should have a corbelled parapet in place of the present modern plain wall. The old design is given by the corbells which remain in the Western bays.

The Cost of carrying out the whole of the Works enumerated will be very great. For this reason I would propose that all fittings should be postponed. The works to the fabric might be divided into several sections, so as to allow a portion being undertaken, if the whole cannot be accomplished. I subjoin approximate estimates for the work in such sections as I think might conveniently be taken, but other modes of division could be adopted on getting tenders from Builders if the Committee should wish to apportion the work differently.

1. The internal repairs to the South Nave and Aisle, including the windows,
   roofs and ceilings   £4960
2. The paving and floors to same   £ 840
3. The external repairs to the same   £ 500
4. The Apse   £2170
5. The Porch   £ 370
6. The Tower   £2450
7. The Parapet &c. to Norman Nave   £ 450
8. The Seats and other fittings   £2300
                                              £14040

Besides these, further sums will be required for warming, lighting — Organ, Architect, and incidental expenses.

I would add that the great interest attached to your venerable Church both from its historical associations and its intrinsic worth, render it well worthy of the large expenditure which must necessarily be involved in putting 'the holy and beautiful house where our fathers worshipped' into such a condition as befits the high purposes for which it was originally built and still continues to be used.

I am, Gentlemen,
Your very faithful servant.
Geo: Gilbert Scott

July 1875.

Fortunately some of Scott's original plans have survived in the collection of the RIBA and two of them are reproduced here. They include the suggested Apse and the proposed seating plan.

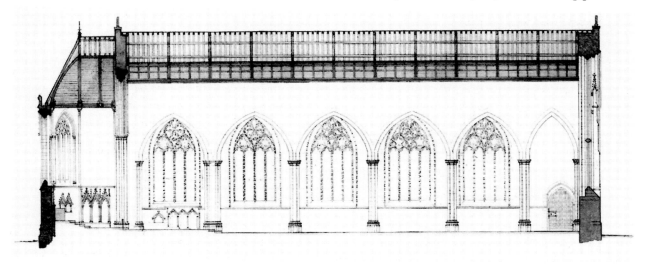

Scott's proposed elevation showing the apse

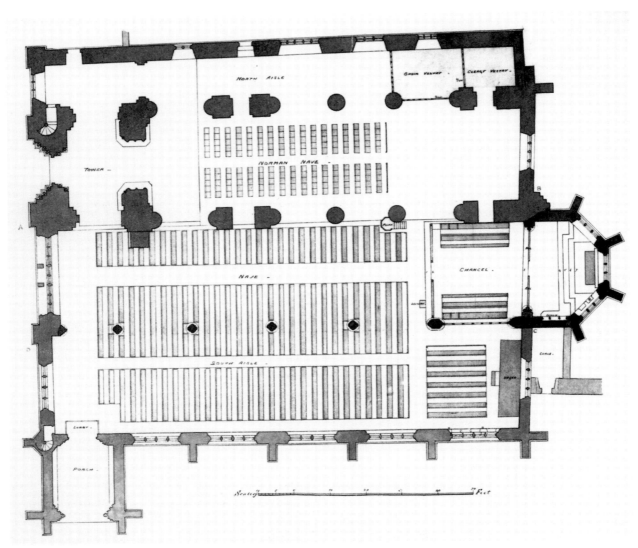

Scott's proposed plan showing the apse and proposed seating arrangements

The first part of the work, mainly the restoration of the Parish Nave but without the proposed apse, was put out to tender, the successful bidder being Charles Edwards, Builder & Contractor of Mill Street, Leominster, who agreed to do the work for £3,300. A Memorandum of Agreement was drawn up between the Vicar, the Churchwardens and the Restoration Committee and Charles Edwards dated June 17th, 1876. A printed form from Sir George's office was used which included the following clause:-

> The whole of the works to be in every respect under the direction of Sir George Gilbert Scott of Spring Gardens in the Parish of St. Martin in the Fields in the Liberty of Westminster in the County of Middlesex Architect and to be executed and completed to his entire satisfaction his decision being final and conclusive in every question which may arise in respect of the said Drawings Specifications & General Conditions and Regulations and of this Agreement.

The completion date was agreed to be August 1st, 1877 with a penalty for unjustified delays of £6 per week.

Fund raising continued and in 1877 Sir George Gilbert Scott wrote an open letter which was published in the *Hereford Times* and the *Hereford Journal* as well as being printed and distributed separately. In it he gives a brief history of the church and then goes on to the real purpose of the letter, an appeal for funds to repair the windows of the South Aisle.

It is the windows of the last-named part to which I desire to call attention.

They are six in number; five to the south and one to the west. The latter having been repaired some years back, I will confine my observations to the former.

They are on a grand scale, and each contains four lights. The whole and each of its halves is subdivided into two arches, each supporting a circle. The smaller circles are exquisitely cusped, while the larger are each divided into three cusped triangles, and three cusped vesicæ. The whole of the mouldings, whether of jambs, arches, tracery, or cuspings, are studied with the ball-flower, giving the whole a most rich and gemmed effect.

Mr. Freeman, in his book on 'Window Tracery,' speaks of this as 'the splendid windows at Leominster, so remarkable for the gorgeous display of ball-flower alike on jambs, mullions, and tracery bars.' In his paper on Leominster in the 'Archæologia Cambrensis' (Jan, 1853), he speaks of this aisle as built 'in the form of singular magnificence, being, in fact, one of the noblest examples in existence of that (the late geometrical) variety of Gothic architecture;' and again he says, 'but the glory of this period is the south side of the church, with its series of five magnificent windows,' and speaking of the profuse use of the ball-flower, he remarks 'the lavish use of this beautiful enrichment seems to be a localism of Gloucestershire and Herefordshire, in illustration of which, I may refer to the south aisle of the nave at Gloucester, to the central tower of Hereford Cathedral (the architecture of which is now just falling into ruin), and to the windows of the chapel on the north side of Ledbury Church.'

Now, the condition of these splendid windows is *simply deplorable*. Two of them long since became so ruinous that as Mr. Freeman says, they 'were shorn of their magnificent tracery in 1812, and common intersecting mullions substituted.' The other three are fast falling into the same state of ruin, and are almost incapable of retaining their glazing, while the mullion of one of them has recently fallen and left the shattered tracery suspended upon its ironwork.

There is, however, enough left to give the exact design of every part, and to supply the actual ancient material for a good deal. If, however, they are allowed to go on unrepaired, not only will it be impossible to use this part (nearly one third) of the church, but the exquisite remains will very shortly fall and become things of the past.

I appeal, therefore, to the county and diocese of Hereford to come to the rescue, and not to allow this right glorious series of windows to perish!

I believe the vicar — full of zeal for his work — appeals by letter to every man of position in the county, and, in return, rarely obtains one word of reply, and still more rarely any pecuniary help! Surely such a fact is a crying disgrace to a great and aristocratic county. *Let the stigma be wiped away ! !*

GEORGE GILBERT SCOTT

March 27th, 1877

Sir George Gilbert Scott died exactly one year later.

In 1878 Rev. Edouart addressed a letter to the members of the Royal Archaeological Institute of Great Britain and Ireland. After describing what had been done and the large expenditure involved he continued:-

> For the rest of this work, in which the late Sir Gilbert Scott was specially interested, and who, but for his lamented death, would have materially aided my efforts, I have no funds in hand, and it is with the view of being able to proceed with it at the earliest period possible, that I throw myself upon your generosity.
>
> To raise the enormous sum of £12,000 still required in a parish where, with but one or two exceptions, there are no resident landed gentry, it is an utter impossibility, to say nothing of the unreasonableness of expecting such a thing.
>
> I am therefore compelled to make this appeal, in the full hope that the most beautiful part of so noble and venerable a building as Leominster Priory Church, an object, too, of such great interest ecclesiastically and architecturally, will not be allowed, for want of seasonable aid, to lapse into irreparable decay.
>
> The late excellent and revered Archdeacon Freer, alluding to the restoration of Leominster Church, speaks of it in one of his charges as 'vying almost with our Cathedral in the grandeur of its dimensions and the beauty of its architecture.' And in his last charge, speaking on the same subject, observes that 'an edifice such as this belongs not to Leominster alone, nor to our county, but the nation, and it is to be hoped that so great a work as its restoration will be looked upon as a national undertaking. ... And I venture to commend the work to the pious bounty of those who desire to be remembered for their zeal towards the House of God, and their love for that place where His honour dwelleth.
>
> I have the honour to be, my lords, ladies, and gentlemen, your humble servant.
> A.G. Edouart, M.A.
> Vicar of Leominster

A subscription list published in 1878 (see opposite and overleaf) contains more than 250 names including The Lord Bishop of Hereford, £100; Brazenose College, Oxford, (a local landowner) £40; The Right Hon. Earl Powis, £25; Rev. Sir F.A.G. Ouseley, Bart. (founder of St. Michael's College, Tenbury Wells), £15. 15s.; and Rev. Sir H.W. Baker, Bart., deceased, £10. The death of the last named meant that they had been deprived of their honorary committee member and active supporter. The largest subscriber was once again John Hungerford Arkwright of Hampton Court with £300, in addition to which he organized a concert in his house which raised £42 17s. 2d. Subscriptions from members of the Royal Archaeological Institute of Great Britain and Ireland were starred and totalled £88. The amount raised at that time was well over £4,000, but the amount required was stated to be £16,000.

Restoration of Leominster Parish Church.

Committee:
THE REVEREND THE VICAR.
Messrs. Churchwardens BANNISTER and STALLARD.

C. D. ANDREWS, Esq.	J. HARDING, Esq.	J. MANWARING, Esq.
W. DAGGS, Esq.	T. W. LANE, Esq.	T. TOOGOOD, Esq.
T. GRAVES, Esq.	E. LLOYD, Esq.	Mr. J. WOOLLEY.

Treasurer: W. DAGGS, Esq. Joint Hon. Secretaries: { THE VICAR. / EDWIN LLOYD, Esq.

Amount of Subscriptions already promised £4,685 1s. 2d.
Amount paid up with Interest on the same £4,031 11s. 4d.
Amount required, 16,000.

Names marked thus * are Members of the Royal Archæological Institute of Great Britain and Ireland.

	£	s.	d.
Hereford Diocesan Church Building Society	100	0	0
Legacy per Executors of the late E. Manwaring, Esq.	400	0	0
The Vicar	50	0	0
The Lord Bishop of Hereford	100	0	0
J. H. Arkwright, Esq.	300	0	0
T. W. Lane, Esq.	200	0	0
J. Manwaring, Esq.	200	0	0
Miss Manwaring	200	0	0
R. Arkwright, Esq.	100	0	0
Mrs. E. C. Hancocks	100	0	0
Henry Herbert, Esq.	100	0	0
Jas. Rankin, Esq.	100	0	0
E. Russell, Esq., deceased	100	0	0
Thomas Sale, Esq.	100	0	0
T. B. Stallard, Esq.	100	0	0
R. W. Evans, Esq.	60	0	0
J. Bevan, Esq.	50	0	0
Rev. H. R. Davies	50	0	0
Mr. C. Edwards	50	0	0
T. Graves, Esq.	50	0	0
Right Hon. Viscount Cranbrook	50	0	0
J. Harding, Esq.	50	0	0
John Jackson, Esq.	50	0	0
Edwin Lloyd, Esq.	50	0	0
The Misses Sale	50	0	0
*H. Webb, Esq.	50	0	0
E. W. Coleman, Esq.	40	0	0
Brazenose College, Oxford	40	0	0
Mrs. J. Marshall	30	0	0
The Right Hon. Earl Powis	25	0	0
C. D. Andrews, Esq.	25	0	0
John Bellow and Son	25	0	0
Rev. Sir E. H. V. Colt, Bart.	25	0	0
Wm. Connop, Esq.	25	0	0
D. F. Davis, Esq.	25	0	0
W. Daggs, Esq.	25	0	0
The Misses Elrington	25	0	0
Mrs. M. V. Guise	25	0	0
V. W. Holmes, Esq.	25	0	0
Miss James	25	0	0
The Misses Timbury	25	0	0
The Rt. Hon. Archdeacon Lord Saye & Sele	21	0	0
Mr Churchwarden Bannister	20	0	0
Mrs. Bevan, Ludlow	20	0	0
Charles Blundell, Esq.	20	0	0
W. S. Boyce, Esq.	20	0	0
Miss Bridgewater	20	0	0
*Jas. Hilton, Esq.	20	0	0
Mr. Huxley	20	0	0
G. T. Robinson, Esq.	20	0	0
E. C. Scarlet, Esq.	20	0	0
Mr William Stanway	20	0	0
F. M. Woodhouse, Esq.	20	0	0
Rev. Sir F. G. A. Ouseley, Bart.	15	15	0
Mrs. Toogood	15	0	0
The Misses Winnall	15	15	0
Mr. Jonathan Meredith, deceased	12	0	0
The Right Hon. the Earl of Meath	10	0	0
The Hon. & Very Rev. the Dean of Hereford	10	0	0
Judge Smith, Q.C.	10	10	0
Rev. Sir. H. W. Baker, Bart., deceased	10	0	0
Rev. H. Arkwright	10	10	0
James Bedford, Esq.	10	0	0
H. Chadwick, Esq.	10	0	0
B. Caldwall, Esq.	10	0	0
Mrs. A. Carwardine, deceased	10	0	0
John Clowes, Esq.	10	0	0
Mr. J. Cox, the Grange	10	0	0
Revd. Prebendary Crouch	10	0	0
Mr. W. J. Davis	10	0	0
„ F. Davis	10	0	0
Mrs. Edouart	10	0	0
Mr. S. Goode	10	0	0
Miss A. Griffiths	10	0	0

	£	s.	d.
Mr. R. Hayes	10	0	0
W. E. Hyde, Esq.	10	0	0
Miss H. N. Hyde	10	0	0
Rev. J. P. Jones	10	0	0
Mrs. D. Lloyd	10	0	0
Mr. Lucas	10	0	0
G. Moffatt, Esq., deceased	10	0	0
T. C Parry, Esq.	10	0	0
H. Pentland, Esq., M.D.	10	0	0
Mr. W. W. Phillips	10	0	0
Mrs. A. Smith	10	0	0
Mr. Thomas Toogood	10	0	0
„ H. Turner	10	0	0
The Misses Watling	10	0	0
Mr. Charles Weaver	10	0	0
J. L. Wight, Esq.	10	0	0
Mr. E. A. Williams	10	10	0
Mrs. James Woodhouse	10	0	0
Mr John Woolley	10	0	0
Rev. Prebendary Hill	7	0	0
Mr. Thomas Meredith	6	0	0
Miss Yeld	6	0	0
Mrs. Allen	5	0	0
„ H. Beavan	5	0	0
Mr. John Bedford	5	0	0
Mrs. Bellow	5	0	0
Mr. W. R. Berkeley	5	0	0
„ J. Blomer, deceased	5	5	0
„ W. A. Boucher	5	5	0
„ F. Bradford	5	0	0
M. Bradley, Esq	5	0	0
Mr E. Bridgwater, deceased	5	0	0
H. G. Bull, Esq., M.D	5	5	0
*H. Bull, Esq	5	0	0
Mr. E Cave	5	0	0
„ William Cross	5	0	0
M. Curtler, Esq.	5	5	0
Mr. William Drew	5	0	0
„ Thomas Dykes	5	0	0
„ M. J. Ellwood	5	0	0
Rev. Prebendary Edwards	5	0	0
Evans, Mrs.	5	0	0
The Lady Emily Foley	5	0	0
Freer Lane, Mrs., deceased	5	0	0
Mr. Froysell	5	0	0
W. Gammidge, Esq.	5	0	0
Mr. W. J. Geaussent	5	0	0
E. Gregg, Esq.	5	0	0
Major Griffiths	5	0	0
Miss Hammond	5	0	0
Honb. & Revd. Prebendary Hanbury	5	0	0
Honb. Mrs. Hanbury	5	0	0
Mr. George Hinton	5	0	0
„ James Irvine	5	0	0
Miss Jones	5	0	0
Rev. C Kent	5	0	0
Mr. J. Lockett, deceased	5	0	0
„ J. G. Lulman	5	0	0
*Archdeacon Maddison	5	0	0
Mrs. Mainwaring	5	0	0
Mrs. Marriott	5	0	0
Meredith, J. Esq.	5	0	0
Mrs. Morris	5	0	0
Mr. Thomas Preece	5	0	0
„ Samuel Price	5	0	0
Miss Pyefinch	5	0	0
James Rankin, Esq.	5	0	0
Mrs. Reynolds	5	0	0
Mr. J. A. Rogers	5	5	0
„ C. J. Saxby	5	0	0
„ F. G. Saxby	5	0	0
Miss Shenton	5	0	0
Mr. E. Smith	5	0	0
Smythies, Geo., Esq.	5	0	0
Mr. Charles Thomas	5	0	0
Mrs. Turner	5	0	0

The Subscription List of 1878

	£	s.	d.		£	s.	d.
Mr. C. E. Turner	5	5	0	*Rev. J. J. Brooke	1	0	0
Mrs. Underwood	5	0	0	Rev. L. E. Brown	1	1	0
Mr. W. Wall	5	0	0	J. A. Carwardine, Esq.	1	0	0
,, John Weaver	5	0	0	Mr. J. Coleman (Senior), deceased	1	1	0
Mrs. Weare	5	5	0	Mr. James Coleman	1	0	0
J. Webb, Esq.	5	0	0	Cook, Son & Co.	1	0	0
Mr. J. West	5	0	0	Copestake, Moore & Co.	1	1	0
Mrs. White, deceased	5	0	0	Crocker, Sons & Co	1	1	0
Mr. J. A. White	5	0	0	Revd E. Davies	1	1	0
Revd. R H. Williams	5	0	0	Mrs. Davies	1	1	0
Mr. James Wilkes (junior)	5	0	0	Miss M. Dent	1	1	0
,, Alfred Witcomb	5	0	0	Miss Dickson	1	0	0
*R. Wood, Esq.	5	0	0	Mrs. Du Buisson	1	0	0
Mrs. J. G. Woodhouse	5	0	0	Rev. J Dudley	1	1	0
Mr. James Baker	3	0	0	J. F Fothergill, Esq.	1	1	0
,, S. L Coxall	3	0	0	Revd J. J. G. Graham	1	1	0
,, E Gunnell	3	0	0	Mr. James Greenhouse	1	0	0
Mrs. Knill	3	0	0	E Hall, Esq.	1	1	0
Mr. J. Langford	3	0	0	B. J. Harris. Esq.	1	1	0
B. St. John Matthews, Esq.	3	3	0	Mr. John Jay	1	0	0
Dowager Lady Shakerley	3	0	0	,, George Johnson	1	0	0
Mr. John Baylis	2	2	0	Lieut.-Col. Money Kyrle	1	0	0
,, T. J. Bannister	2	2	0	* D. Laing. Esq	1	0	0
Mrs. Bannister (Weston)	2	2	0	Mr. R. R. Miles	1	0	0
,, Redward	2	2	0	Revd. E. Palin	1	1	0
,, S. Bird	2	2	0	Mr. H. Parsons	1	0	0
Mr. George Blacklock	2	2	0	Revd. A. Pope	1	1	0
,, S. Geaussent	2	2	0	Mr. William Poulton	1	0	0
,, T. Ingram	2	0	0	Mrs. Price	1	0	0
,, Robert Jones	2	2	0	Mr. William Price	1	0	0
Leaf, Sons & Co.	2	2	0	,, Thomas Pritchard	1	0	0
Mr. W. Lewis	2	2	0	,, Thomas Ravenhill	1	0	0
,, Thomas Lloyd	2	2	0	,, John Rogers	1	0	0
Miss Marshall	2	0	0	J. B Rose, Esq.	1	1	0
Mr. William Mason	2	2	0	Mrs. S. Southall	1	0	0
Potters & Norris	2	0	0	,, M. W. Taylor	1	0	0
Rev. Prebendary Phillott	2	0	0	Wm. Taylor, Esq.	1	1	0
Mr. Thomas Smith	2	2	0	Walsh, Captain, R.A.	1	0	0
,, William Turner	2	2	0	Revd. T. W. Webb	1	0	0
Rev. J. M. Ware	2	0	0	Mrs. Wells	1	0	0
Rev. W. Wyatt	2	2	0	Subscriptions under One Pound	7	18	10
Miss Fletcher	1	10	0	Balance from last Church Restoration Account	2	14	0
*Rev. Sir. T. Baker, Bart.	1	0	0	Proceeds of Concert, per J. H. Arkwright Esq	42	17	2
Anonymous	1	0	0	Interest on deposits	82	7	11
Mrs. M. A. Baker	1	0	0	Sale of Sermon	4	0	0
H. C. Beddoe, Esq	1	1	0	Church Box	19	1	0
Revd. G. A. Blakely	1	0	0				
Boddington, Miss	1	1	0				
Mr. F. E. Bradley	1	1	0				

	£	s.	d.		£	s.	d.	£	s.	d.
Card per The Lady Mary Arkwright	10	10	0	Card per Jones, Mrs.	1	9	0			
,, C D. Andrews, Esq.	10	0	0	,, Levine, Miss C.	4	0	0			
,, Baker, Miss A.	1	6	0	,, Lloyd, Mrs. D.	2	18	0			
,, Baker, Miss	1	0	0	,, Pyefinch, Miss	1	0	0			
,, Beavan, Miss	1	0	0	,, Roberts, Miss	3	16	0			
,, Bannister, Mrs	10	0	0	,, Rudge, Miss	1	0	0			
,, Bellow, Mrs	1	5	3	,, Russell, Miss	23	5	0			
,, Daggs, Miss	11	1	0	,, Sale, the Misses	18	3	0			
,, Davis, Mrs, D. F.	1	0	0	,, Urry, Miss	3	0	0			
,, Edouart, Mrs	6	2	6	,, Weaver, Mrs. C.	1	13	0			
,, Ellwood, Mrs	30	17	0	,, Wells, Mrs.	1	0	0			
,, Foreman, Miss	2	0	0	,, Mrs. J. W. West	2	0	0			
,, Geaussent, Mrs W. J.	1	10	0	,, Miss West	1	10	0			
,, Gilkes, Mrs.	1	17	6	,, Winnall, Miss L.	1	0	9			
,, Gilkes, Miss A.	3	0	0	,, Winnall, Pupils of Miss	3	6	2			
,, Mrs. Henry	1	15	6	,, Woodhouse, Miss	9	3	3			
,, Homfray, Miss C.	7	0	0	,, Woodhouse, Miss M.	15	0	0			
,, Irvine, Miss	2	10	0	,, Woodhouse, Miss C.	2	0	0			
Jones, J. A. Esq., B.A.	2	10	0	Cards under One Pound	2	16	6			
								£208	11	5

Subscriptions and Donations may be paid in to the account of the Treasurer of the Leominster Parish Church Restoration Fund at the Leominster Branch of the Worcester City and County Bank.

JULY 18th, 1878.

The Subscription List of 1878

CHAPTER 7
PROGRESS AT LAST: THE PARISH NAVE — 1875–1876

The contract with Charles Edwards specified 'the South Nave of the Priory Church at Leominster', which I have been calling the 'Parish Nave'. However the work actually covered most of the nave and some of the South Aisle. This was due to the urgency with which some repairs and restoration were required.

One of the early decisions was to postpone the building of the Chancel Apse on account of its cost, but with this exception the work followed the plans drawn by Sir George Gilbert Scott in 1875.

The arcade between the Parish Nave and the South Aisle was virtually rebuilt. In addition to more slender columns an extra arch was opened at the eastern end, the whole of this leading to better visibility from the aisle to the nave. The lead roofs of both were recast and a new ceiling was erected over the nave. Oak flooring was put down in the Parish Nave with the passages laid with coloured tiles, and the eastern end of the nave paved with encaustic tiles, supplied from Mr. Godwin's Encaustic Tile Works, at Lugwardine. The chancel part of the nave was raised above the general floor level and paved with encaustic tiles. The oak screen and fittings were removed from the Norman to the Parish nave and considerably improved.

There was a lot of work required to repair the stonework damaged by the building of the several galleries. While the west wall of the Parish Nave was being repaired a discovery was made which Rev. Edouart later described:

> Upon opening the Arch immediately under the Great West Window, the fresco of an encircled nondescript cross was discovered on the plastered wall at the back, of which I had a careful tracing taken, the plaster being in so perishable a condition that the wall was obliged to be re-plastered, an exact copy of the cross from the tracing, being at the same time painted on the precise spot of the original one. The history of this cross, according to the late Sir George Gilbert Scott's version, is that it was placed there at the time of the Consecration of the Church, and was (as was usual in those days) blessed by the Bishop. Underneath, is a pavement of ancient encaustic tiles found in the Norman Nave, probably part of the High Altar.

The great west window was thoroughly restored and the two middle lights filled with stained glass in memory of the late Mr. John Arkwright, the work being done by Herr Meyer of Munich at a cost of £250. This was due to a proposal by Councillor Gunnell during his mayorality in 1876 to commemorate a munificent patron of the Priory Church as his son, the new owner of Hampton Court, had proved to be many times since then. It was paid for by subscription. They would like to have filled the whole window with stained glass, but the cost of nearly £1,000 was too great.

In the end only some of the windows were restored. The western window of the Parish Nave was fully restored, as described above, but the eastern window, which was built in the 18th century, seems to have required little attention.

The South Sisle has seven windows. The one in the east end was of the 18th century and, like its counterpart in the Parish Nave, seems to have required little attention. The rest were the ball-flower decorated windows referred to by Sir George Gilbert Scott in his letter, there being five in the south wall and one in the west. Two of these windows had fallen out and been rather crudely replaced in 1812. The easternmost window in the south wall was fully restored, the work being carried out by Mr. Edwards using stone from a Luston quarry belonging to Capt. Scarlet and said to be of excellent quality. It was glazed with Cathedral-tinted glass by Mr. Poulton, of Leominster. No mention is made of the window in the west wall of the South Aisle.

The total expenditure on the work of restoration was £8,543 10s. leaving a deficit of about £600.

The Parish Nave restored, the South Aisle untouched (sometime between 1879 and 1885)

The Parish Nave was reopened on May 29th, 1879. The proceedings comprised early communion at 8 a.m., morning service at 11, with a sermon by the Bishop of Hereford, a public luncheon at 1 p.m., with the Mayor of Leominster in the chair, and afternoon service at 3.30 p.m., with a sermon by Lord Saye and Sele, Archdeacon of Hereford.

During the speeches after the lunch, which was held in the Town Hall, the Lord Bishop of Hereford remarked that when he stood in the pulpit that day, and looked down the South Aisle, with the rubbish accumulating on the floor, it was suggested most convincingly to his mind that at all events before long that floor must be put in a proper state. The Parish Nave was only separated from its aisle by a wooden partition some four or five feet in height. It was to be many years before the restoration of the South Aisle was completed.

Mr. Edwin Lloyd while proposing the toast of 'the Bishop and Clergy of the Diocese', mentioned the fact that three members of the Restoration Committee had died since the last similar gathering. These were Rev. Sir Henry Baker, vicar of Monkland, Rev. Edward Evans, a wealthy clergyman of Eyton Lodge, and Rev. G.T. Whitfield, rector of Pudlestone, the last two had also been members of the original Restoration Committee.

A rather curious letter was published in the *Hereford Times* on June 7th, 1879:

Leominster Priory Church
To the Editor of the Hereford Times

SIR,— The full and interesting report you have given in the Hereford Times of today of the re-opening of the south nave of the Leominster Priory Church winds up with a list of contributors. As this is presumably supplied by the treasurers of the restoration fund, and contains amounts down to £8, I am at a loss to know why the name of the borough member has been omitted. It was probably an oversight, but as Mr. Blake, though a Nonconformist, did actually contribute £25 it is unfair to him, as well as to the Liberals of Leominster, that the amount should be ignored, while smaller amounts are publicly acknowledged.

Leominster, May 31st, 1879   A LIBERAL

There was a comment in the newspaper report of the services on the occasion of the re-opening of the Parish Nave that the organ was still in the North Aisle and too far separated from the choir. One of the first decisions taken even before the general restoration had been agreed was that the organ should be moved to the east end of the South Aisle and is shown in this position on Scott's plan of 1875. The removal of the organ to this position was delayed by lack of funds and the fact that the restoration of the South Aisle had not been completed. As the Lord Bishop of Hereford had remarked, the floor had not been re-laid and was covered with rubbish. Fortunately the new arcade had been completed and an extra arch opened at the east end, near to the new site for the organ. Also the easternmost ball-flower window in the south wall had been restored. However, work was still required to make good the damage done to the east wall of the South Aisle by the building of the gallery.

Charles Edwards, who had made an excellent job of restoring the Parish Nave, undertook to restore the east end of the South Aisle for the sum of £84, Mr. Percival Vernon of Hereford being the superintendent architect, and Mr. Nicholson, of Worcester, consented to remove the organ and to thoroughly tune it for £35. A subscription list was opened, the work being completed by the beginning of August, 1883. This had not been without its opponents, especially when the subscription list was opened in March. One of several anonymous correspondents who signed themselves as 'Churchmen' complained that as the finances of the Church were 'in a hopeless muddle' and that there was insufficient money to meet regular expenses or to repay the treasurer of the Curates' Fund who was out of pocket, it was hardly the time to solicit funds for moving the organ.

On August 14th a special service was held in the Priory Church to celebrate the move. The sermon was preached by Rev. A.T. Peppercorn, Rector of Stoke Prior, and the organ was played by W.H. Richmond, Esq., Organist and Director of the Choir of St Michael's, Exeter.

That same evening a concert was given in the Corn Exchange Hall in Leominster in aid of the organ fund.

A further window in the south wall was restored in 1884 at a cost of £367 10s.

CHAPTER 8
THE SOUTH AISLE AND PORCH: 1875–1876

Yet another public meeting was held in the Town Hall on August 4th, 1885 in order to raise funds for the completion of the restoration. Once again the Bishop of Hereford presided but most of the speaking was left to Rev. Edouart. He gave a description of how the church looked when he arrived in Leominster in 1862, part of which has been quoted above, but most of the time he talked about money.

This was not surprising for the financial situation of the Priory Church had got even worse. In January that year the regular columnist in the *Leominster News* who wrote under the name 'Liliputian' had made some interesting comments about a change in the way the church collected the offertory. This was the replacement of the closed bags with open plates so that the donors would be aware that others could see the size of their donation and be ashamed to put too little on the plate. He then wrote: 'Alas, too true it is, that men will wrangle for their religion — write for it, and in solitary instances, fight and die for it. But how few, (I am speaking now of the Church of England in this town) are willing to pay for it.' The following week Lilliputian noted that the church had been unable to pay the organist.

Rev. Edouart lamented the passing of several benefactors including Mr. Robert Lane of the Ryelands, Mr. Thomas Sale, the solicitor, both members of the original committee, Mr. Herbert and Mrs. Hancock, supporters whose places had not been filled up. He also mentioned the current depression in trade.

The late 1870s saw the beginning of a general depression, and agriculture, on which Herefordshire depended for much of its livelihood, suffered particularly. Not only were there a series of bad harvests but 1873 saw the beginning of a rise in grain imports from the USA, and by 1885 improvements in refrigeration had led to increased competition in the livestock market from producers in Australia, New Zealand and Argentina. The general fall in agricultural incomes affected everyone, but especially the large land-owners such as Lord Bateman of Shobdon Court, Lord Rodney of Berrington Hall, and John Hungerford Arkwright of Hampton Court. Lord Bateman appeared in the Bankruptcy Court in 1895 and Lord Rodney tried to sell the Berrington Estate in 1887 but only succeeded in selling a small part, there being very little market for agricultural land. Mr. Arkwright managed to hang on but soon after his death in 1905 his son, John Stanhope Arkwright, began to sell that estate. The Leominster properties were sold in 1907 and the rest of the estate by 1912. At the time John Hungerford Arkwright became Lord Lieutenant of Herefordshire in 1901 he confessed himself to be penniless, but he had been short of money for some time as is shown by some correspondence in 1886 that will be considered later.

1885-6 was a rather turbulent time politically and there were General Elections in November 1885 and July 1886. At the first of these the Liberals got the largest number of members without getting an overall majority so the government did not change until Lord Salisbury resigned in January and Gladstone took over, relying on the support of the 86 Irish Home-Rulers. James Rankin, the Conservative member for Leominster lost his seat to Thomas Duckham, the Liberal candidate, much to the alarm of Rev. Edouart. This was because the Liberals were thought to support the disestablishment of the Church of England and Rev. Edouart was a firm anti-disestablishmentarian. In a New Year sermon preached on the afternoon of the first Sunday in January, 1886, he claimed that 'the church was threatened with disestablishment and disendowment, and the empire and constitution with almost total overthrow; and this too, by a body of unscrupulous statesmen who by false promises and false representations were determined to pursue and to encompass their wicked ends, adopting any means even to the selling of their own country for the attainment of their purposes.'

This was evidence of the split in the town between the Conservative Church and the Liberal Non-conformists which made it even more difficult to obtain new subscriptions for the next phase

The South Aisle after restoration in 1886, and before the new east window of 1889

of restoration. However money was collected and on December 22nd, 1885, articles of agreement were signed between the restoration committee and Charles Edwards for the restoration of the South Aisle, porch and windows adjoining, and the lowering of the ground outside. F. Robert Kempson was the architect.

Work commenced in January. New floors were laid down similar to those in the nave with oak for the main floor and aisles of Godwin's encaustic tiles. The plaster ceiling was removed and replaced with one of oak with moulded ribs. The walls were repaired, especially where the stone steps to the galleries had been removed, and the masonry pointed.

The porch required a lot of work. The floor was lowered by about three feet, bringing it to its original level. It had been approached by a flight of steps, but these were no longer necessary. All the decayed stone was cut out and the buttresses, bases, etc., renewed. The earth outside the porch was also lowered by some three feet, exposing the bases of the buttresses. The roof of the porch was restored being re-leaded and with a new ceiling made of oak with moulded ribs. The porch was floored with Godwin's encaustic tiles, and the old doors replaced by iron gates supplied by Messrs. Leatherin, of Cheltenham.

Another of the windows in the south wall was restored and re-glazed with cathedral tinted glass. This only left the two windows crudely rebuilt in 1812 to be restored to their former glory at a future date.

The earth along the west end of the church was cleared away to a depth of between two and three feet and the headstones of the graves there placed horizontally on the new level.

The paths approaching the porch were lowered to avoid the need for steps to reach the lowered floor. In the course of these excavations a large number of human bones were discovered and their

The South Aisle sometime shortly before 1890

condition, as well as their nearness to the surface, led to the assumption that these were persons slain during the Civil War. It was believed that the addition of a mound of earth to the west of the Church that led to the need for its reduction along the west wall was due to the construction of a battery of three guns by the Parliamentarians.

The work was completed by November, and on November 16th, 1886, services of re-dedication were held. The sermon at the morning service was preached by the Lord Bishop of Hereford, and that in the afternoon by Rev. Sir F.A.G. Ouseley, Bart., who had taken an active interest in the restoration. At the morning service the Vicar gave to the church as a thank offering a handsome pulpit gas stand, and Mrs. Edouart presented an enamelled jewelled altar cross.

CHAPTER 9
COMPLETED? 1886–1889

The following correspondence has survived in the Arkwright archives. It comprises two letters from Rev. A.G. Edouart and the rough copies of the replies from John Hungerford Arkwright, Esq. The fact that they are rough means that we cannot be absolutely certain about the form of the final versions, but it is fairly certain that they did not differ greatly.

The Vicarage, Leominster
Dec. 6th, 1886

My dear Sir,

The <u>whole</u> restoration of Leominster Priory Church being now completed and the portion recently restored, rededicated on <u>16th ulto.</u> I trust you will now see your way to fulfil your promise made in a letter bearing date <u>October 18th</u> of <u>last</u> year of paying the £100 still due, either by <u>instalment</u> or otherwise, <u>which</u> ever may best suit your <u>convenience</u>. I very reluctantly press for payment of this sum, but the Committee I regret to say, are responsible for near upon £600, for which they will have to pay <u>£5 per Cent</u>, which is a serious consideration.

   Allow me to remind you that the terms under which you promised your subscription of £1000 was that the <u>Norman Nave</u> should be restored <u>instead</u> of the <u>Church</u> in which public worship was then conducted, and that the services of the late Sir G. G. Scott should be engaged for that purpose, which nave was reopened after restoration in <u>1866</u>.

I am My dear Sir

Very truly yours

J. H. Arkwright Esq.   A. G. Edouart

The underlining is Edouart's own.

   There are several points of interest in this letter. The first is that Rev. Edouart considers the restoration complete despite the fact that two of the windows in the south wall were still in the rather crude state of their repair in 1812, and that parts of the tower were in danger of collapse. Then there is the dissatisfaction Edouart obviously felt both about the employment of Sir G.G. Scott and the fact that it had been decided to begin with the restoration of the Norman Nave instead of the Parish Nave, thus delaying the restoration of the latter by some fifteen years.

   The draft reply is difficult to decipher in places but it probably reads:-

I need hardly repeat what I have said so often before that it is my intention to pay as soon as I possibly can the remaining portion of my subscription to the Priory Church. It was promised on the condition that the whole work was done and I thought at the time that it was quite(?) my share of the whole cost. Since that each year has shewn me that I had no right whatever to have given anything approaching that sum as(?) I have never had five shillings in my life to call my own since schoolboy days. However having(?) promised I mean to perform

JHA

P.S. I will give you a note of hand if you like.

This elicited the following reply:-

The Vicarage, Leominster
Dec. 11th 1886

Dear Sir

If, as I infer from the tone of your answer, my letter of <u>6th</u> inst has given offence, I am truly sorry.

The '<u>whole work</u>' of restoration is now accomplished, but if by '<u>whole work</u>' you mean the restoration of the <u>outer fabric</u>, then allow me to say, that such a thing was not at the time you promised your donation, spoken of, nor has it <u>ever</u> been, or is it <u>now</u> <u>contemplated</u>.

So far as I am concerned, your <u>note of hand</u> for the outstanding £100 of your subscription is not required.

J. H. Arkwright Esq.   A. G. Edouart

The draft of Arkwright's reply is written in pencil on a blank portion of Edouart's second letter.

Dec 12

I am not the least offended — but thought it was necessary to explain further than had been done before the cause of my not paying up.

JHA

As has been mentioned above, there was an agricultural depression that affected Herefordshire in general and Leominster in particular which had begun around 1879. Before that date there were numerous building projects completed in Leominster including the New Town Hall in 1855, the Savings Bank in 1857, the Corn Exchange in 1858-9, the new building for the National School in 1858, the Weslyan Methodist Church in 1861, the new building for the British School in 1862, the Congregational Church in Burgess Street in 1867-8, the new town water supply and drainage in 1867, the Primitive Methodist Church in 1873, the Orphans' Home in 1873, and the rebuilding of Hester Clarke's Almshouses in 1874. There were also the railways of North Herefordshire which were completed by 1877 with the exception of the Leominster to Bromyard section of the Leominster to Worcester line, which was an exception in more ways than one.

In Leintwardine in 1871 a union of farm labourers was established, led by Thomas Strange, a schoolmaster in the Primitive Methodist school there. It was named the North Herefordshire and South Shropshire Agricultural Labourers' Improvement Society and it later became part of the National Agricultural Labourers' Union, led by Joseph Arch, who at one time had worked on the Arkwright estate of Hampton Court. Agricultural wages had stagnated owing to the drop in the price of agricultural produce being 11s. 9d. in 1879, 11s. in 1892, and 12s. 8d. in 1898. A knock-on effect of this was an increase of poverty in Leominster. This had become so bad that in 1888 a special Soup and Coal Fund was set up, funded by charitable people in the town and neighbourhood. £85 16s. was raised and the organizers were able to serve hot soup and to distribute 1,896 cwts. of coal, 4,040 loaves of bread and 1,667 lbs. of meat. This was the economic climate in which Rev. Edouart was attempting to raise money.

In 1887 there was considerable discussion in Leominster about how to celebrate Queen Victoria's Golden Jubilee. Money was collected and it was agreed at a public meeting that it should be spent on a general celebration with a dinner in Broad Street. The Vicar was one of the few who opposed this idea and suggested that it should be spent on something more permanent, such as the apse at the east end of the Parish Nave, or a stained glass window. Nobody agreed so Rev. Edouart and Mr. C. Edwards decided to erect a screen for the South Aisle at their own expense. It was dedicated in February, 1888 with a plaque which read:-

> To the glory of God and in commemoration of the Jubilee of Victoria, England's beloved Queen, June 20, 1887. This screen is the joint gift of A.G. Edouart, M.A. Vicar of this parish and C.E. Edwards, builder, who carried out the restoration of the central and south nave of the church.

The sermon at the dedication was preached by Rev. T. Peppercorn in which he mentioned the desirability of the apse and the restoration of the tower.

To make matters worse one of the most important members of the Restoration Committee died suddenly on April 15th, 1888 at the age of 72. His obituary appeared in the Leominster Deanery Magazine:

THE LATE MR. EDWIN LLOYD– This respected gentleman breathed his last at his residence in South Street, on Sunday morning, April 15th, after only four hours' illness, at the ripe age of 72 years. For fifty years he practised as a Solicitor in this town, and in addition filled several public as well as private offices. He was a warm supporter of the National Schools, acting as Hon. Sec. to the School Committee, and was besides a liberal contributor towards the restoration of the noble Priory Church. A staunch Conservative in politics, he was also a loyal and attached member of the Church. He was interred on April 19th, in a vault in the Priory Churchyard, originally built for the remains of his son, Percy Lloyd. The funeral procession, which was very large, was joined at the Town Hall by the Mayor and members of the Corporation, Mr. Lloyd having for many years served the office of Borough Treasurer, shop shutters being up and blinds drawn throughout the whole route. The burial service was conducted by Rev. A.G. Edouart, the Vicar of the parish, and the church choir took part, singing at the grave's side the deceased's favourite hymn, 'For ever with the Lord' (Hymns Ancient and Modern, 231). On the Sunday morning following, the Vicar preached a funeral sermon, taking for his text, Ecclesiastes ix. 5, clause 1st, 'For the living know that they shall die'.

The anonymous author of a *History of Leominster National Schools*, published in the *Leominster News* in 1900, said:-

> He was intensely interested in all educational matters, and had, as Hon. Sec. [of the National School], rendered invaluable service to the schools. He was devoted to his labours, liberal in support, wise in council. In fact the success of the schools to a large extent was due to his interest and influence. Throughout the lengthened period of his work as Secretary he had been one of the most generous supporters, leading the way in every time of special appeal, and as an evidence of his general sympathy with the work of education in the town may be mentioned that he was for many years a subscriber also to the British Schools.

To compound problems his death occurred at a time when the Vicar, having called a Vestry meeting to consider the outstanding Church debt of some £44 was confronted by a request that he open his pulpit to visiting preachers. Rev. Edouart was completely against this fairly common practice. 'I will not suffer my pulpit to be used at the dictation of my congregation.' he said, and did not come to the meeting as he thought that the petitioners would threaten to withhold their financial support unless he gave way. Mr. F.G. Saxby, one of the principal petitioners commented that he was 'sorry to see so little sympathy between congregation and minister'.

One piece of restoration was carried out privately more than a year later at a cost of £1,000, namely that of the central window in the South Aisle:

> In loving memory of my Father Captain William Elrington and my sister Catherine Elrington of this Borough this window was erected by me Francis Elrington.
> October 1889

CHAPTER 10
THE TOWER: 1890–1891

Despite Rev. Edouart's claims the restoration of the Priory Church was far from complete. As far back as Mr. Scott's report issued in August 1862 attention had been drawn to the state of the tower, parts of which were said to be in a dangerous condition. In his second report dated July 1875 Scott stated: 'In my former Report I directed attention to the very serious condition of much of the Stonework, and the lapse of thirteen years has greatly increased the extent of the dilapidations. ... The tower parapet has been so weakened by decay that one side has actually been blown down and a second side has had to be removed to avoid a like fate.'

It was not until 1890 that tenders were invited for the repair of the tower. The tenders received were:

Mr. Millward (Leominster)	£2,000
Mr. Edwards (Leominster)	£1,470
Messrs Jones and Son (Sedgeley)	£1,400
Mr. Collins (Tewkesbury)	£1,365

A meeting of the Restoration Committee was called for the 24th June, 1890 to consider the matter. The Vicar revealed that only £700 had been subscribed and still less had been collected, and he admitted that it was becoming harder and harder to collect funds for this project. The Mayor, Mr. T.B. Stallard,. said that the tower was in a dangerous state and work should begin at once, but when Rev. Edouart asked if he was prepared to make up the required sum, he replied 'Certainly not; but it's no use waiting until it falls down.' Rev. Horton of Ivington commented that 'If we wait till it falls down upon us there will be no subscribers left.' After considerable discussion it was decided that restoration should begin at once.

A letter from Mr. Edwards dated the same date as the day when the committee had opened the tenders was then read in which he explained that he had committed a miscalculation in preparing the tender, and reducing his tender by £129 to £1,341. Mr. John Woolley, the postmaster, moved that they should ignore that letter and accept Mr. Collins's tender, while the Vicar moved an amendment that they accept the revised tender from Mr. Edwards. The amendment was carried and Edwards's contract was declared accepted.

The appointment of a clerk of works, and the question as to when the work should commence, was left to Mr. Kempson, the architect, who was present at the committee meeting. He engaged Mr. J. Martin as Clerk of Works, a man of considerable experience in church restoration.

The structure of the tower is complicated. The western bay of the Norman building was not designed to have a tower, although there are differences between it and the remaining bays of the nave. It is claimed that the west door was a later addition, although nearly contemporary with the rest. The height of the original west front was no greater than the subsequent extensions comprising the magnificent doorway and the Norman window above it.

Only when they built the South Aisle in the 14th century did they feel the need for a west tower. They were aware that the existing work at the west end of the Norman Nave would be insufficiently strong to support the additional weight of the tower they wanted, but they wished to preserve the existing west door and the window over it, so piers and arches were constructed within the westernmost bay of the nave without taking down any of the Norman arches except perhaps one which probably spanned the nave between the east piers and the painted side arches which form the western bay of the Norman nave arcade. The 14th-century piers and arches were carried up within, and partly on, the old Norman work, with the result that when the new work subsided a little it created collateral damage to the existing structure. To make matters worse the stone used was of inferior quality being very friable. The buttresses at the four corners of the tower were never properly bonded to the tower and became detached in places, and were subsequently bound up to the walls by iron bands so that the tower supported the buttresses instead of the other

The north side of the church c.1866-1890 showing evidence of collapsed battlements on the tower

way round. The iron bands had given way and when the buttresses were rebuilt, care was taken to bond them firmly with the stonework of the tower. The new buttresses were made slightly larger than the old.

There were numerous cracks in the stonework of the tower over the windows and elsewhere, and when some of the stones in the old Norman masonry at the base of the tower were removed in order to repair the cracks, it was found that the interior consisted of loose stones, so that the whole weight of the tower rested on the outer facing only. The cracks were washed out and a special prepared mixture of liquid cement with the consistency of glycerine was poured into the interior of the walls, some of which percolated down as much as 20 or 30 feet below the point at which it was poured in. It eventually took a total of 40 tons of the mixture to fill up the cracks.

It proved easier to rebuild the ashlar work on the north and west sides of the tower. The cracks were strengthened by the introduction of hard, flat bedded bonding stones across the openings. The stone was obtained from the best quarry in Luston, probably that which has been referred to earlier as belonging to Captain Scarlet. The mortar was made from lias lime, made by an approved manufacturer, and sharp well-washed sand.

The Vicarage and Church Street in the 1880s, again showing evidence of collapsed battlements on the tower

Great pains were taken to restore the tower to its original state in every detail, the Restoration Committee wishing to follow Sir G.G. Scott's belief in 'restoration' rather than 'improvement'. After the battlements and pinnacles had been taken down the best preserved specimens were re-erected in the churchyard, and carefully sketched by Mr. Martin, who also prepared full size detail drawings of all the mouldings tracery, carving, etc., which had to be removed. The work was done slowly to give time for the new masonry to settle down gently. However Mr. Martin stated in March that he still expected the work to be finished by the stipulated date, namely August, 1891. It was not to be, and the *Leominster News* published the following report:

September 4th, 1891

A meeting of the Leominster Church Restoration Committee was held on Monday, when there were present: The Rev. R. Horton, Messrs C.D. Andrews, T. Bannister, C. Weaver, G.T.P. Robinson and the secretary the Rev. G.W. Whitehouse. In the absence of the Vicar, Mr. C.D. Andrews was elected to the chair. A letter was received from the architect (Mr. F.R. Kempson), in which he said he had ordered a weather-cock, to cost £12 10s., with the cardinal points and cock gilded complete. The architect's monthly report stated that the roof was now being re-covered with lead, and the work above the roof line was finished. Little now remained for the contractor to do, except the windows, which were partly prepared. Progress had been slow, but the work was standing very well. The architect further added that it would not be wise to allow bell-ringing until the bells were properly re-hung. He also pointed out the condition of the west window of the south nave, the mullion of which was split by the frost the previous winter.

To complicate matters Rev. Edouart was suffering the re-occurrence or worsening of the eye trouble that had prevented him from accepting the bishopric of Sierra Leone some forty years before. The *Leominster News* reported the progress of his illness.

October 2nd, 1891

We regret to hear that the Vicar, the Rev. A. G. Edouart, M. A., is still suffering from his eyes, and though a little improvement was reported yesterday, he will be permitted, we understand, to exert them but little in any public duty for some time. It is said that Dr. Lindsey has advised an operation, but whether it will take place or not we do not know. The Vicar's health, apart from the painful affection of his eyes, is remarkably good. The pulpit on Sunday last was again occupied by the curate, the Rev. G. Whitehouse.

October 9th, 1891

The Vicar, we are glad to hear, is a little better. The improvement, though slight, encourages the hope that he will be allowed to go out in the mornings shortly, but he will not be able to venture out at night for some time to come.

October 23rd, 1891

The Vicar of Leominster, we are glad to say, was able to resume ministerial duty last Sunday morning, and preached again. He dwelt very forcibly on the 'Perilous times' in which we live, but the discourse was somewhat pessimistic in tone.

CHAPTER 11
THE BELLS: 1891–1894

There were almost certainly bells in the church from early times, possibly in the central tower, but the first positive mention is in connection with the 1397 Visitation: 'The parishioners say that the parish clerk is not able to ring the bells at the hours, as he is bound, because the monks have custody of the key.' This was probably part of the same friction between the Priory and the Parish that had led to the building of the Parish Nave. Another early reference is in 1458 when William Reynold of Leominster bequeathed 6s. 8d. for the new bells, probably for the newly heightened tower. The inventory of 1553 shows that there were five bells, while that for 1620 lists seven, plus 'one littell sunrice bell'.

The bell ringers were paid. They received 10d. for one important occasion in 1558, together with bread and ale to the value of 8d. The amounts vary. For welcoming the accession of Queen Elizabeth they received 6d., while for the celebration of the defeat of the Armada they received 2s. 6d. On several occasions they received money for beer.

The fire of 1699 caused considerable damage, but the bells were saved. When the church was restored they built a new ringers' floor below the level of the Norman west window, thus hiding it from view from the interior of the church. In 1745 one of the bells was reported cracked, but nothing was done for the next ten years when negotiations began for the re-casting of the bells. The two competing tenders were from Mr. Wm. Evans of Chepstow, and Mr. Abel Rudhall of Gloucester. It was the former who won the contract but Mr. Rudhall was paid £2 2s. to cover his expenses and loss of time. The bells were conveyed to Chepstow, leaving Leominster by barge on the River Lugg, which had recently been made navigable. The cost was £216 16s. for the recasting, and Robert Pennie was paid £15 1s. for freight charges.

In 1848 the vestry refused to pay £1 to repair the chimes and £34 to rehang the bells. This caused considerable complaint and further proposals were made, but it was not until December 1850 that the work was put in hand. In March 1851 the *Hereford Journal* stated: 'Mr. John Wall, bell-hanger of this town, conducted the iron-work department upon a superior and scientific system, whereby greater harmony and richness of sound is perceived. Mr. Page, builder, superintended the timber work.' In actual fact the bells seem to have been hung by Francis Woodhouse, an ironmonger and wholesale seed merchant. Soon after this the floor of the ringing chamber was removed and the bells were then rung from the floor above. Unfortunately the bells did not remain ringable for very long for in 1888 it was reported that there were no ringers and the bells were out of order.

At the meeting of the Restoration Committee on July 7th, 1891 the report on the state of the bells by Taylor and Sons, of Loughborough was considered. This stated: 'All the bells appear sound and good, but are becoming worn at those places where the clappers strike, and require quarter-turning in their head-stocks, so that the clappers may strike on the fresh places. They are not quite perfectly in tune, the smaller bells being rather too sharp, but there is very little in the matter. The fittings, *i.e.* the wheels, headstocks, gudgeons, clappers, etc., are in a very dilapidated condition, and thoroughly worn out, and must be entirely renewed before the bells can be in safe ringing order again. The framework also should be entirely renewed, for it is not only too tall, and on that account rickety, but is altogether much too light. It appears to be *extremely old and decayed,* and I think most of the timbers, by the appearance of the mortice holes, etc., were formerly part of the frame for the bells before they were re-cast in 1755.' Mr. Taylor considered it dangerous to have even one bell rung. The estimate for renewing the framework of the bells and other repairs was £283 9s.

Rev. Edouart remarked that he had been told that the bells were in a dangerous condition when he arrived in Leominster nearly thirty years earlier, but had ordered the bells to be rung. They had been ringing without trouble until the present and he thought they could be rung for another thirty years. Mr. Charles Weaver, a boot and shoe manufacturer of 1, Draper's Lane and a member of the restoration committee, told them that as an old bell-ringer he considered that there was no imminent danger. He also drew attention to the fact that the framework was not fixed to the walls of the tower.

Another member of the committee, Mr. Charles Moore, a solicitor, drew attention to the fact that in the event of any accident occurring, the committee would be held to blame for allowing them to be rung after expert opinion was against it. The matter was dropped owing to the lack of the necessary funds.

Mr. Moore's warning must have been taken to heart for the committee had the bells examined by Messrs. Warner of London, and Messrs. Llewellyn and James, of Bristol, both of whom agreed with the above report but thought they could be restored for about £200. As a result the bells were silenced, much to the annoyance of one parishioner, Mr. Edwin Gregg, a solicitor who lived in the Lighthouse on the banks of the River Kenwater not far from the Priory, and who was clerk to the guardians and superintendent registrar of births, marriages and deaths. He wrote a letter to the *Leominster News* in January 1892 complaining of their silence over Christmas and the New Year. Rev. George Whitehouse, the Curate of Leominster and Hon. Sec. of the Restoration Committee replied at length explaining the position. He concluded by reminding people that the Hon. Treasurer, Mr. E.P. Bowen (Manager of Lloyds Bank in Leominster) would be thankful to receive contributions towards the cost of restoration. He also suggested that it would be an excellent opportunity for Mr. Gregg to 'shew his appreciation of the music of the bells of his parish church, by placing his name and donation at the head of the list, when doubtless many of his fellow parishioners would follow his example, which would be much more useful than the empty precept, or complaints at the silence of the bells.'

As ever fund raising was an ongoing problem. At a special meeting held in Leominster Town Hall in May 1893 and presided over by Archdeacon Stanhope of Hereford supported by Rev. the Hon. A.A.B. Hanbury, the rural dean, it was pointed out that there was still a deficit of £506 12s. outstanding in the general restoration account. The Archdeacon lamented the disappearance of

Church rates and mentioned a threatened attack upon the Church of England, both of which made it more difficult to obtain financial support.

Rev. Edouart listed some of the ways in which money had been obtained. Some £3,518 8s. 7d. had been contributed by outsiders; £910 had come from legacies; entertainments by Mr. Arkwright and other friends had realised £105 0s. 2d; the church box brought in £146 6s. 7d; the proceeds of the bazaar, pamphlets, sale of work, etc. came to £357 17s. 9d; the Diocesan Church Building Society contributed £220; offertories, exclusive of those at the re-opening, amounted to £375 18s. There had also been collections taken at the Cathedral and various Parish Churches. By the end of the meeting the Archdeacon was able to state that the debt was now reduced by donations and promises by £224.

The effects of the agricultural depression were still being felt. The same May 26th edition of the *Leominster News* that had contained a report on the public meeting in the Town Hall had, on its front page, an advertisement for materials for farm buildings was headed: AGRICULTURAL DEPRESSION.

An editorial note beginning 'In these days of depression ...' contained the information that Colonel Cox of Broxwood Court and Rev. R. Evans of Eyton had returned ten percent of the rents to their tenants.

In April 1894, by which time the debt had been reduced to about £94, another bazaar and jumble sale was organised under the patronage of, among others, Lord and Lady Bateman of Shobdon Court, a new name among the list of supporters. It was held in the Corn Exchange where there was a Fancy Stall, an Old-Clothes Stall, a Flower Stall a Book Stall, an Ironmongery Stall and a second Fancy Stall specially for collecting funds for the restoration of the Church bells. Half-hour concerts were given in one of the side offices with vocalists and instrumental selections. The newspaper account also mentions 'Clever ventriloquial entertainments were also given, by arrangement by Prof. Delmar and other members of a company now in the town.' Mr. Mayor's band was also in attendance. Mr. Mayor was a music teacher and the Church organist.

About £140 was raised, including £34 by the stall for the restoration of the bells, so the balance of the main debt was cleared. Soon after, Messrs. Warner and Sons of London were contracted to carry out the restoration of the bells.

Their contract not only included the re-casting and re-hanging of the existing bells, but the addition of two treble bells bearing the date and names of the Vicar and the two churchwardens (Messrs. T. Bannister and T.B. Stallard). There was great local pride in the fact that Leominster Priory Church now possessed the only 'ringable' peal of ten bells in the Diocese of Hereford, those at the Cathedral being almost 'unringable'. The new frame was of oak and the ropes were specially made by Messrs. Ironmonger of Wolverhampton.

Mr. H. Reeves, of London, the editor of the *Bell News* had made a report on the bells and recommended an additional two, suggesting the removal of the 'cumbrous works of the ancient clock, which took up a great deal of unnecessary occupied space in the belfry.' Mr. Reeves also composed a peal of 6,000 changes to be rung to celebrate the dedication of the new bells.

The ringers comprised T.J. Bratton (Welshpool), treble; T. Russam (Birmingham), 2; S. Reeves (West Bromwich), 3; W.R. Small (Tipton), 4; F.E. Ward (Cheltenham), 5; J.S. Pritchett (Kings Norton), 6; J. Carter (Birmingham), 7; J. George (Rugby), 8; J. Ashbury (Walsall), 9; W.H. Fussell

LEOMINSTER PRIORY CHURCH
DEDICATION OF THE NEW BELLS

and services in connection with the

RE-HANGING of the FINE OLD PEAL
TUESDAY, NOVEMBER 20TH, 1894

12.30 p.m. – DEDICATION OF NEW BELLS
7.0 p.m. – FESTAL EVENSONG

Preacher: THE RIGHT REV. THE BISHOP OF SHREWSBURY

From 1 to 4 p.m., a PEAL of 6000 CHANGES will be rung by an
ALL-ENGLAND COMPANY of SCIENTIFIC RINGERS

A COLD LUNCHEON provided at the Royal Oak Hotel at 2/- each.

(Slough), tenor. The ringing was conducted by Mr. John Carter. The ringers were to have rung a peal of 6,000 changes, on the principle of Stedman but, unfortunately, after 5,000 changes had been rung the ringer of the tenor became somewhat indisposed, and, therefore, the conductor wisely shortened the performance bringing his bells home after 5,295 changes.

The evening service was a full festal evensong, and the whole church was crowded. The presence of the Bishop of Shrewsbury (Sir L.L.T. Stamer, D.D., Bart.) was explained by the ill-health of the Bishop of Hereford. There was a civic procession headed by the Mayor and Corporation and the choir was specially augmented for the occasion by members of the Presteign choir.

After the service, the ringers dined with the curate and the composer of the peal at Mrs. Vearnall's Temperance Hotel.

CHAPTER 12
THE END OF AN ERA: 1896

Rev. Augustin Gaspard Edouart had been experiencing difficulties with his sight as early as the 1850s, when he declined the bishopric of Sierra Leone for this reason, but by 1894 it had become so bad that could no longer occupy the pulpit. On May 2nd, 1896 the *Leominster News* reported rumours of his resignation which was formally announced just over a week later.

An appreciation of him and his work, together with a brief biography, was published in the paper on May 15th, 1896 one paragraph of which is particularly worth quoting.

> The lengthy incumbency of the Rev. A.G. Edouart at Leominster presents many features of general and ecclesiastical interest, but only one or two can be indicated in this article. The Vicar entered upon his work [in Leominster] *con amore*, and his zeal soon made itself felt in many directions. An earnest and consistent Churchman, with moderately High Church views, he attracted a large congregation. His sermons were of an exceptional merit; many revealing the firm grasp of the theologian, and all possessed the literary flavour of one whose reading was extensive. Discourses, alike admirable in style and spirit, graphic, and charged with much feeling, often lingered in the memory. That some of the utterances of so strong a Churchman should be open to criticism was not surprising, and his occasional sermons touching political and ecclesiastical questions provoked no little feeling. Those, however, emphasised the position that he had always held as a Churchman, and showed the essential differences of standpoint taken by him and those who were opposed to him on such questions. The preacher could speak 'with words that burn,' and, without defending such words, it will be readily admitted that they left no doubt as to his attitude, sincerity, and courage.

The resignation was not due to take effect until September but in May a petition in favour of the appointment of the curate, Rev. George Whitehouse, as the new Vicar, signed by more than 1,000 parishioners, had been forwarded to the Lord Chancellor. The curate had been in Leominster for seven years and had been in virtual charge during the previous two years when the Vicar's deteriorating health had prevented him from fulfilling his normal duties.

However, the Rev. Whitehouse was not the only applicant for the vacant appointment and, despite the wishes of a large number of the parishioners, it was Rev. James Hamilton Charles who was appointed. It is interesting to note that Rev. Charles had only been seven years old when Rev. Edouart came to Leominster.

The Mayor of Leominster, Councillor Andrew Duncan, organised a collection and at a ceremony in the Town Hall at the end of September Rev. Edouart was presented with an Illuminated Address in album form with a list of subscribers, and a purse of £100. Much attention was drawn to the enormous labour he had undertaken in the restoration of the Priory Church. Dr. Hyde, a councillor and local surgeon, commented: 'Unfortunately for a few years past the Vicar had not been in a position, owing to a painful affliction, to take an active part in the services and work of the Church, but nothing had been left undone by his curate to carry out the duties in a satisfactory manner, and it must have been a good thing for him to have such a good helper'.

In his reply Rev. Edouart told his listeners that he had written some 20,000 letters in his attempts to raise funds for the restoration. He would start each day by writing six letters but only one in ten received an answer. Contributions varied from one shilling to £500.

Rev. Whitehouse's name was not included in the list of those present for the presentation.

On Monday, 5th October, another Presentation took place in the Town Hall. Once again this was organized by the Mayor, but this time it was Rev. Whitehouse who was honoured. The *Leominster News* noted that 'The Town Hall was filled with a large gathering representing all classes, socially and religiously, Nonconformists as well as Church People taking the opportunity of showing the universal esteem in which Mr. Whitehouse had been held'. A suitably inscribed clock was given by the members of the Communicants Guild and the Mayor commented that it would remind him of the many lady friends he left behind in Leominster. This was in addition to the gift of an Illuminated Address and list of subscribers, with a purse of 90 guineas. The list contained the names of 173 subscribers as opposed to 94 in the list for Rev. Edouart. In his closing remarks the Mayor commented on the success of Rev. Whitehouse in 'bringing Church people together to an extent that was not the case 15 or 20 years ago.'

The name of Rev. Edouart was not included in the list of those present.

On October 30th the Bishop of Hereford inducted the new Vicar, Rev. James H. Charles, aged 41. He had been Vicar in the parish of Whittlesey St. Andrew (near Peterborough) for ten years, having previously been Curate of Eastham, Cheshire.

Rev. Edouart retired to Nyanza Villa, Grange Park, Ealing where he died on 14th March, 1905, aged 88. The obituary published in the *Leominster News* contained the following comment::

> Some of his discourses as a churchman, called forth considerable criticism, his views being regarded as narrow and intolerant; while his occasional sermons on political and ecclesiastical questions of the day provoked a good deal of bitter feeling. These, however, emphasised the positions he had always held, and showed the essential difference of standpoint taken by him, and those opposed to his views. There was no doubt at any rate about his attitude, sincerity and courage, and it must not be supposed that his sermons were of these kinds. The ordinary discourse was often admirable in spirit and in style, and marked by true insight, feeling and force.
>
> The Vicar loved the Priory Church.

This last remark was certainly true and if it had not been for his tenacity, courage, and sheer hard work, it is doubtful whether Leominster Priory Church would have survived in the form we see it today.

CHAPTER 13
TIDYING UP: 1896–1902

Rev. Charles, the new vicar, entered into a church whose appearance contrasted very favourably with that found by his predecessor in 1862. It was true that it was awkwardly divided into two parts, one being the Norman Nave and the other the Parish Nave with its South Aisle, but the latter had benefited by the changes to the arcade dividing the nave from the aisle and the whole had a fresh, new look about it. True, there was still an un-restored window in the south aisle, but the fabric was sound for the first time in more than a hundred years.

The new vicar seems to have been in no hurry to finish the few things his predecessor had left undone, and even when an opportunity occurred in the celebration of the Diamond Jubilee of Queen Victoria and he was appointed to the Jubilee Committee it was left to his wife to make the following appeal:-

> Amongst the many plans and preparations for the commemoration of the Queen's Diamond Jubilee when everyone's heart is full of thankfulness, we feel we would like to place in our Priory Church some standing memorial of God's goodness in prolonging for sixty years the life of so great and good a Queen. There will be so many calls on the liberality of our people that we propose to limit the subscription to 2/6 (of course anyone is at liberty to give more if they desire to do so), and to provide a handsome brass lectern, and if funds permit to get a Bible to place on it. A design of the lectern may be seen on the notice board of the church. The Churchwardens have kindly consented to help me to receive subscriptions, and we should be greatly obliged if all who desire to help will send their subscriptions before June 4th, so that our offering may be placed in the Church by June 20th, the great Thanksgiving Sunday.

This was a very modest request compared to that for a memorial window that had been made by Rev. Edouart on the occasion of the previous jubilee.

In May, 1897 the death was announced of Alderman T.B. Stallard, J.P. He was a successful wine merchant and one of the most respected as well as the senior member of the Borough Council and had been one of the original members of the Restoration Committee. He had been a Churchwarden for most of Rev. Edouart's incumbency.

It was the death of Queen Victoria in 1901 that gave a new impetus to the idea of restoring the remaining window in the South Aisle. The Local Notes column of the *Leominster News* for April 12th, 1901 contained the following entry:-

Easter Vestry Meeting

THE MEMORIAL WINDOW

The Vicar said there was one other matter to which he would like to refer, and that was the proposal that the memorial in Leominster to their late beloved Queen should take the form of the restoration of the South Nave window. A meeting of the committee consisting of the Vicar, the Churchwardens, sidesmen, Mr. J.H. Arkwright and the Mayor, would be held next Tuesday, at 12 o'clock, to consider the steps to be taken with a view of raising the necessary amount. He had received a letter from Mr. Arkwright intimating that he hoped to attend.

There were two letters in the next edition of the newspaper stating similar views.

MEMORIAL TO QUEEN VICTORIA
To the Editor of the Leominster News.

Sir.- In your report of the Easter Vestry meeting last week there is reference made to a memorial to our late Queen ; and in the Deanery Magazine for April it is assumed 'that it has now become an accepted fact that the memorial in Leominster should take the form of the restoration of the only un-restored window, and of some beautiful stained glass treatment in it of our Lord's Nativity.' It is estimated that this will cost something like £800, and it is further assumed that 'every inhabitant of the ancient and loyal borough of Leominster will desire to help in establishing this beautiful and permanent memorial to the Queen in the old mother church of the town and neighbourhood.'

Now all this looks as though the promoters of the scheme, viz., the Vicar and Churchwardens, wished it to be regarded as a public, town's memorial, whereas, as a matter of fact, the townspeople have never been consulted, nor have they had any voice whatever in the matter. If the Vicar and Churchwardens are anxious to get a new window in the priory Church, and like to solicit subscriptions from those who are interested in its adornment, by all means let them do so; no one has any right to object. At the same time it is just possible that the inhabitants of Leominster, if they entertain the idea of a memorial at all, might find some better way of spending £800 for the benefit of the whole town than by placing an ornamental window in the parish church, which will benefit no one, and will gratify only a small proportion of the community.

The idea of a public memorial in memory of Queen Victoria is in itself a good one, but in order to give proper effect to it, let a public meeting be called in the Town Hall, and let the townspeople themselves determine the form it shall take – whether a fund for the endowment of the Cottage Hospital, Public Baths, a Public Recreation Ground, or any other object which shall be for the general good of the whole town. – I am yours,

PRO BONO PUBLICO.

A second, similar, letter, written from Leominster and dated April 18th, 1901 concludes:- 'Is not the placing of a coloured window in the parish Church, costing £800 rather a matter for a churchman's beneficence than for a Borough memorial scheme?' and was signed 'Yours faithfully. OBSERVER'.

In the same edition there was a report of the meeting of the Committee.

A meeting of the Committee of the 'Queen Victoria Memorial Window' Fund and consisting of the Vicar, Churchwardens, and Sidesmen, the Mayor (Councillor A. Lewis), and Mr. J.H. Arkwright, was held in the vestry on Tuesday morning. The Rev. J.H. Charles, who occupied the chair, briefly explained the scheme for the restoration of the South Nave window, and it was resolved to at once take steps to raise the necessary funds by sending circulars to the residents of the town and neighbourhood, and to all likely to be interested in the scheme, and by opening lists at each of the Banks where subscriptions might be paid. It was considered desirable to extend the constitution of the Committee, and with this view the Rev. D.A. Brown and Mr. F.G. Blacklock were elected as members, power being reserved to still further add to the number. Mr. V.W. Holmes undertook the duties of Hon Treasurer, and Mr. W. Elsmere those of Hon. Secretary. A sum of £50 is already available, including a contribution of £25 from Sir James Rankin, M.P.

The two additions to the committee are very significant. Rev. D.A. Brown had begun his ministry in the Congregational Church in Burgess Street in Leominster in 1879 and was a well-respected figure in the town. Mr. Frank Gainsford Blacklock was the son of the manager of the Orphan's Printing Press which had been founded by the local Quakers as a means of providing training and work for the boys from the Leominster Orphanage. He was a convert to Catholicism and had founded the Mortimer Press and published his own excellent history of Leominster entitled *The Suppressed Benedictine Minster and other Ancient and Modern Institutions of the Borough of Leominster* in 1897.

Two months later the newspaper reported as follows:-

June 14

A circular in the interests of the Queen Victoria Window in the Priory Church has been issued by the Committee, and it is hoped that the appeal will meet with a generous response. It is intended to restore the only un-restored window in the South Nave and to fill it with glass representing 'The Nativity of Christ.' It is calculated that a sum of about £850 must be raised to carry out the scheme, and there is every confidence that the required amount will be contributed. Such a confidence is based upon the following, among other reasons: (1) the Church is a venerable historic building of which the town justly boasts; (2) the work is in every way desirable, and the window ought to be in accord with the other four windows; (3) the fact that the scheme is a Memorial to Queen Victoria is in itself an appeal; and (4) that while the work has a special claim on Churchmen, it is such as to interest every resident in the town. A subscription list has been opened, contributors being able to extend their contributions over two years, and the Committee hope soon to be in the position to report the satisfactory progress of the fund.

The first report on July 5th shows that subscriptions had reached £157 2s. 6d., but by the end of 1902 a total of £700 had been collected and it was decided that they could go ahead. Detailed specifications for the stonework were requested from Messrs. Thompson & Co., of Peterborough, and designs for the glass from Mr. Kempe of London. The window was completed by the middle of 1903 using stone from the Wrexham quarries and was unveiled at a service held on July 25th. The unveiling was performed by the Lord Lieutenant of Herefordshire, John Hungerford Arkwright.

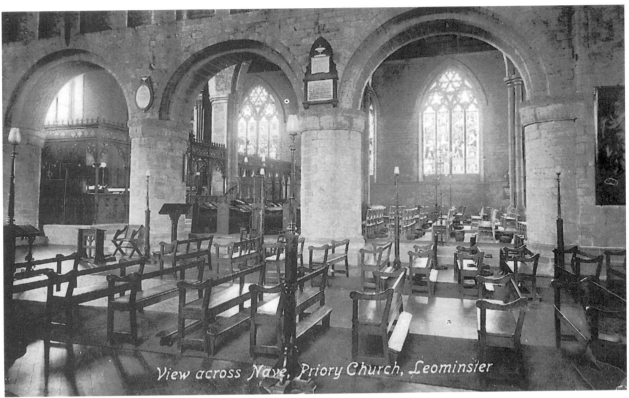

View across Nave, Priory Church, Leominster

This could not have been more appropriate for not only was he the representative of the Queen's successor, King Edward VII, but he was also one of the last surviving members of the original Church Restoration Committee. With the restoration of this window the tasks set out in the report by Mr. G.G. Scott in August, 1862 had been completed. A brass plate beneath the window is inscribed:-

> To the Glory of God the King of Kings in pious memory of Victoria our Queen, who reigned over the British Empire for sixty three years 1837 to 1901. This window is restored and dedicated by her loving subjects the people of Leominster and their friends.

CHAPTER 14
AND FINALLY? 1920

The restoration of the window in the South Aisle completed the restoration of Leominster Priory as envisaged by Rev. A.G. Edouart, Sir George Gilbert Scott, and John Hungerford Arkwright, Esq. some forty years earlier. It had taken far longer and cost far more than they had originally envisaged but there was general agreement that the effort had been worthwhile. Mr. Arkwright had become Lord Lieutenant of Herefordshire in 1901 and maintained his interest in the Priory to the end. Both he and Rev. Edouart died in 1905.

The one rather glaring omission from the plans for restoration were the three east windows which had been restored in the 18th century.

In 1920 the Diocesan Architects (Messrs. Nicholson and Clarke) were called upon to make a report on the state of the church. Their report in January 1921 was not a happy one. It would seem that the repairs to the South Aisle in the 1880s had not gone far enough, especially as regards the exterior of the walls. In particular the buttresses and battlements of the South Front needed

An aerial view (taken from 500 feet) of the Priory church in September 1920

urgent attention although the restored windows were given a reasonably good bill of health. This was not the case with the east window of the South Aisle, reported as being: 'In a very perished and somewhat dangerous condition, the jambs, mullions, and portions of the tracery being crumbled away and before long the mullions may collapse.' The west window of the South Aisle also needed some attention. The total cost was initially estimated to be £2,250 but this was later increased.

The suggestion was made that the work should be done in sections, as it had been done before, but fortunately Mr. Andrew Duncan, an ironfounder and ex-Mayor, offered to donate 10% of the total cost, provided it was done in a continuous fashion, but only £100 if it was done in sections, so a single contract was agreed to and his donation was formalised at £300.

In May, 1922 it was agreed that the east window in the Parish Nave should be replaced as part of further repairs to the church. The sum of £900 had been given in memory of the widow of Mr. Colt for a window to commemorate the Colt family. They no longer lived in Leominster but one member in particular had been prominent in the history of the town. He had been MP for Leominster with only a short break from 1678 to 1698 and lived in Dutton House, then called Stafferton House, in the centre of Leominster. He was an outspoken opponent of the Duke of York and was found guilty of high treason in a trial before Judge Jefferies in May 1684. Damages were assessed at £100,000 and he was committed to prison. He delayed his arrest by concealing himself in a hiding place in a chimney of Dutton House, but eventually gave himself up. The window was dedicated on September 8th, 1922. The stained glass is by Kempe and Towers.

In April, 1934, it was decided that the east window of the Norman Nave should be replaced by a replica of the Norman window at the west end of the nave, the architects being Nicholson & Clarke of Hereford.

Of course a building the size of Leominster Priory Church requires almost constant repairs and maintenance but there have been other changes such as a new pulpit erected in memory of a former Vicar, Rev. Edouart, and presented in 1908 by Miss Wood of The Ryelands. The dedication read: 'To the glory of God, and in loved and honoured memory of Augustin Gaspard Edouart, for 35 years Vicar of this parish, by whose devoted energy, under God, the restoration of this Church is due, this pulpit is erected by his friend, Alice A. Wood, Palm Sunday 1908'.

The organ was overhauled in 1948-50 and a new console placed on the opposite side of the Parish Nave, a new Chancel floor laid in 1950, and west doors of Weobley oak hung to commemorate the Coronation of Queen Elizabeth II. These and other minor changes have done little to alter the fact that the church we see today is almost entirely the result of the plans drawn up in 1862.

It is a pity that the apsidal chancel that Sir George planned to add to the Parish Nave was abandoned for financial reasons, but thanks to that dedicated band of people we have a building that can, and has, served a wide variety of purposes. It has served as a recording studio (for the recording of Fauré's *Requiem* by John Eliot Gardiner in 1992), and it has been the site of numerous concerts for the Leominster Festival with soloists such as Marisa Robles, Emma Johnson and Julian Lloyd Webber. Somewhat more surprisingly it has served as a film set for Rik Mayall when he was making his TV series *Violent Nation*.

But it is primarily a place of prayer and worship as it has been for more than 1,300 years. Can we hope that this will continue until at least the next millennium.

Bibliography

Anon *The Priory Church, Leominster. A Brief Survey, Historical and Architectural*, Orphans Press, Leominster, 1920

Beale, Catherine *Champagne and Shamble. The Arkwrights and the Downfall of the Landed Aristocracy*, Sutton Publishing, 2006

Blacklock, F. Gainsford *The Suppressed Benedictine Minster and other Ancient & Modern Institutions of the Borough of Leominster*, The Mortimer Press, 1897 (2nd edition Leominster Folk Museum, 1999)

Brown, Duncan L. & Wilson, Duncan 'Leominster Old Priory: recording of Standing Buildings and Excavations 1979-80', *Archaeological Journal*, **151**, 1954, pp.307-368

Edouart, Rev. A.G., *History Past and Present of the Priory Church of Leominster*, Orphans Press, Leominster, 1879

A Paper on the Priory Church of Leominster, Read before the Members of the Woolhope Naturalists' Field Club on the occasion of their visiting the Church on May 31, 1892, The Mortimer Press, Leominster

Freeman, Edward A, 'Leominster Priory Church' (read at Ludlow), *Archaeologia Cambrensis*, 1852, pp.9-13

'Excavations at Leominster Priory Church', *Archaeologia Cambrensis*, 1853, pp.180-188

Hillaby, Joe 'Early Christian and Pe-Conquest Leominster: An Exploration of the Sources', *Woolhope Club Transactions,* 1987, Part III, pp.557-685

Kempson, F.R. 'The Restoration of the Tower of the Priory Church, Leominster', *Woolhope Club Transactions*, 1892, pp.291-2

Price, John *An Historical & Topographical Account of Leominster and its Vicinity,* Ludlow, 1797

Reeves, Norman C. *The Town in the Marches*, Orphans Press, Leominster, 1972

Rushforth, G. McN. 'The Wheel of Life the Ten Ages of Life in Leominster Church', *Proceedings of the Society of Antiquaries*, second series, Vol. XXVI, 1913/14, pp.47-60

Scott, Sir George Gilbert *Personal and Professional Recollections*, London, 1879 (extended edition Paul Watkins, Stamford, 1995

Smith, Thomas *A Brand Plucked from the Burning: or My Life*, London, 1856 (republished by Leominster Folk Museum with additional material, 1999)

Townsend, Rev. George Fyler *The Town and Borough of Leominster; with illustrations of its Ancient and Modern History*, Leominster, 1862

Williams, Rev. Jonathan *The Leominster Guide: containing an historical and topographical view of the ancient and present state of Leominster*, printed by and for F.J. Burlton, Leominster, 1808 (2nd edition, Leominster Folk Museum, 2000)

Woodiwiss, John *British Silhouettes*, Country Life Ltd., London, 1965

Priory Church Guides (approximate dates only) 1945, 1953, 1955, 1969, 1980, 1999

Newspapers and Periodicals
  Hereford Journal
  Hereford Times
  Leominster News
  Leominster Deanery Magazine

Numerous pamphlets and other short publications published in the last half of the 19th century in the Leominster Museum Collection and in the possession of the author.

Index

Also from Logaston Press

The Churches of Worcestershire
by Tim Bridges

Introductory chapters tell of the spread of Christianity across Worcestershire and the major events that affected church building in the county over the centuries. The core of the book is a gazetteer to the 270 Anglican churches in the county, detailing their building history, furnishings and tombs.

Tim Bridges lectures widely on church architecture and history and works as Collections manager for Worcester City Museums.

ISBN 1 904396 39 9 (978 1 904 396 39 0)
Paperback 288 pages, over 200 illustrations   Price £14.95

The Churches of Shropshire & their Treasures
by John Leonard

This book explores 320 parish churches of Shropshire, half of them medieval. Chapters guide the reader through changing architectural styles, from Anglo-Saxon origins to the 21st century and then detail the treasures of the churches, including towers and spires, porches roofs, sculpture, fonts, memorials and monuments, stained glass, rood-screens, pulpits, pews and chancel furnishings. The county is then divided into geographical areas, with descriptions of all the individual churches in each area.

John Leonard is a retired consultant physician who lives in Shropshire and has written numerous books on churches.

ISBN 1 904396 19 4 (978 1 904 396 19 2)
Paperback 336 pages, over 530 illustrations   Price £12.95

The Churches of Herefordshire & their Treasures
by John Leonard

This book adopts a similar approach to that for Shropshire noted above, but covering Herefordshire.

ISBN 1 873827 91 1 (978 1 873827 91 8)
Paperback 240 pages, 290 illustrations   Price £12.95

Also published by The Friends of Leominster Priory
in association with Logaston Press

Leominster Priory, Minster and Borough, c660–1500
by Joe & Caroline Hillaby

Joe Hillaby combines his extensive knowledge of the early British church, the Saxon minster and subsequent priory with recent research and archaeological excavation and analysis to present a picture of Leominster from the foundation of its minster, c660, and associated borough, c1123, to the priory's dissolution in 1539.

Leominster's church is shown to have been one of the great religious foundations of England, with an important collection of relics, a huge area of pastoral responsibility — its *parochia*, stretching some 18 miles east to west and 12 miles north to south — and similarly extensive estates, managed from four burys or granges at Stockton, Ivington, Luston and Stoke. Although Henry II made the priory subsidiary to his foundation at Reading where he was to be buried, its importance remained.

Chapters consider many aspects of the priory's functions, and its relations with the bishops of Hereford, the townspeople and local congregation. They catalogue the effects of the priory on the borough's location, development and shape, and the subsequent infilling of part of its market area. This is a book that, above all, brings together countless strands to give an understanding of Leominster and its rural hinterland.

ISBN: 1 904396 55 0 (978 1 904396 55 0)

Paperback 320 pages, over 200 black & white and colour illustrations   Price £10